30119 027 050

D1137320

A Copper
at the Yard

TRUE CRIME FROM WHARNCLIFFE

Foul Deeds and Suspicious Deaths Series

Barking, Dagenham & Chadwell Heath	Jersey
Barnet, Finchley and Hendon	Leeds
Barnsley	Leicester
Bath	Lewisham and Deptford
Bedford	Liverpool
Birmingham	London's East End
Black Country	London's West End
Blackburn and Hyndburn	Manchester
Bolton	Mansfield
Bradford	More Foul Deeds Birmingham
Brighton	More Foul Deeds Chesterfield
Bristol	More Foul Deeds Wakefield
Cambridge	Newcastle
Carlisle	Newport
Chesterfield	Norfolk
Colchester	Northampton
Cotswolds, The	Nottingham
Coventry	Oxfordshire
Croydon	Pontefract and Castleford
Derby	Portsmouth
Dublin	Rotherham
Durham	Scunthorpe
Ealing	Shrewsbury and Around Shropshire
Fens, In and Around	Southampton
Folkstone and Dover	Southend-on-Sea
Grimsby	Staffordshire and The Potteries
Guernsey	Stratford and South Warwickshire
Guildford	Tees
Halifax	Uxbridge
Hampstead, Holborn and St Pancras	Warwickshire
Huddersfield	Wigan
Hull	York

OTHER TRUE CRIME BOOKS FROM WHARNCLIFFE

A-Z of London Murders, The	Norwich Murders
A-Z of Yorkshire Murders, The	Plot to Kill Lloyd George
Black Barnsley	Romford Outrage
Brighton Crime and Vice 1800-2000	Strangeways Hanged
Crafty Crooks and Conmen	Unsolved Murders in Victorian &
Durham Executions	Edwardian London
Essex Murders	Unsolved London Murders
Executions & Hangings in Newcastle	Unsolved Norfolk Murders
and Morpeth	Unsolved Yorkshire Murders
Great Hoaxers, Artful Fakers and	Warwickshire's Murderous Women
Cheating Charlatans	Yorkshire Hangmen
Norfolk Mayhem and Murder	Yorkshire's Murderous Women

Please contact us via any of the methods below for more information or a catalogue
WHARNCLIFFE BOOKS
47 Church Street, Barnsley, South Yorkshire, S70 2AS
Tel: 01226 734555 • 734222 • Fax: 01226 734438
email: enquiries@pen-and-sword.co.uk
website: www.wharncliffebooks.co.uk

A COPPER AT THE YARD

Inside the Real Sweeney

John Woodhouse

Foreword by
Former CID Commander Roy Ramm
New Scotland Yard

First Published in Great Britain in 2012 by
Wharncliffe True Crime
an imprint of
Pen and Sword Books Limited,
47 Church Street, Barnsley,
South Yorkshire. S70 2AS

Copyright © John Woodhouse, 2012

ISBN: 978 184563 160 4

The right of John Woodhouse to be identified as author of this work
has been asserted by him in accordance with the Copyright, Designs
and Patents Act, 1988.

A CIP catalogue record of this book is available from the
British Library.

All rights reserved. No part of this book may be reproduced, stored in a
retrieval system   ns, electronic,
mechanical, ph   out the prior
permission in w

Typeset in Plan

Printed and bo
by CPI Group

LONDON BOROUGH OF SUTTON LIBRARY SERVICE (SUT)	
30119 027 050 94 9	
Askews & Holts	May-2013
363.2092	

Pen & Sword B
Pen & Sword A   r Sword
Maritime, Pen   Wharncliffe
Local History, Wharncliffe True Crime, Wharncliffe Transport, Pen &
Sword Select, Pen & Sword Military Classics, Leo Cooper, Remember
When, The Praetorian Press, Seaforth Publishing and Frontline
Publishing

For a complete list of Pen & Sword titles please contact
PEN & SWORD BOOKS LIMITED
47 Church Street, Barnsley, South Yorkshire, S70 2AS England
E-mail: enquiries@pen-and-sword.co.uk
Website: www.pen-and-sword.co.uk

Contents

Foreword

The Bill, *The Sweeney*, *Ashes to Ashes* and a hundred other books and television series about the Met going right back to good old George Dixon all owe something to the thousands of coppers who have shaken countless door handles, smelt the stench of the dead and felt the collars of the living on the streets of London and survived life at the Yard with their heads still on roughly the right way round. Policing London is a continuing story about people like John, of ordinary men and women, doing extraordinary things every day. And whilst the fiction focuses on the drama and comes to us in short, episodic bursts, the reality is that real police officers risking their lives in dangerous undercover operations are also running their own back story of ordinary lives with families, kids, illnesses and ground-floor extensions!

John Woodhouse's career weaved round the streets of East London, of China Town and the corridors of New Scotland Yard then into the offices of the Bomb Squad, Flying Squad and the Intelligence Branch. Whilst Commissioners recount the dizzying heights of their achievements and philosophise about the place of policing in society, John Woodhouse tells a straightforward, but compelling and very funny, personal story of a policeman in society. His is a story that intertwines an account of his battle to overcome a dreadfully serious illness with a determination to make it as a police officer; it is about how 'The Job' eats into your life and consumes your family time; it is about much too much to do and not enough time to do it.

If you don't want to think about what ordinary coppers deliver for Londoners; if you don't want to know what it really feels like to work undercover; if you don't care if your local Chinese restaurant is run by the Triads; or if you are affronted by the Flying Squad morris dancing; and think it is inappropriate for a disabled detective to be nicknamed 'One lung' and to dress up as an ostrich, then don't read anymore. If you don't read on, you'll miss out. Trust me: I'm a police officer!

Roy Ramm
Former Commander, New Scotland Yard
August 2012

Acknowledgements

There comes a time in life when we should take one step back and look at who and what we are, or what we have become, as seen by ourselves and perhaps by others, a kind of life assessment. With some trepidation I took that first step of this self-analysis by putting pen to paper so to speak, but nevertheless this is my story. I hope this literal walk with me down one or two of the many roads in my life will give you an amusing insight into how I see my life, and how grateful I am to so many people whose help and encouragement have made this little bit of fun possible, and for me an enjoyable marathon.

I should mention however that some times, places, and names have been changed to protect the innocent and not so innocent, but the stories themselves are all true to the best of my memory. I should also like to take this opportunity to thank my wife Sue for putting up with me, not only during the writing of this book, but over the past fifty years, God bless her. Also a number of friends who have spent many hours going through the many pages of the book, and of course offering good sound advice, but I still continued writing:

Dick Kirby, ex-Flying Squad officer with a wicked sense of humour
Professor John Shepherd and his wife Janet
Roy Ramm, ex-Commander, New Scotland Yard
Richard North, BEng, MPhil, CEng, MIET, MIPEM, a hippy friend of mine of over thirty years
Ivor Jones, ex-head teacher who can spell.

Prologue

What a start to the day, but cold wet early mornings were becoming the norm these days. I sat there in the back of a old battered Transit van with six other guys waiting for the off, via a radio message from New Scotland Yard to tell us the villains were on their way to our location, but that could be hours yet. I was getting used to life on the Flying Squad, New Scotland Yard's most successful and best known thief-catching squad in history, just sitting in wait, armed to the teeth, well a 2in snub-nose 38 Smith and Western actually, and although quite small, it was digging into my side. These shoulder holsters were very good hiding a gun when standing, but a bugger when sitting in a cramped old van. It was no good, I had to take it out and push it into my coat pocket, so I could relax a bit before world war three started. According to an informant, these villains we were expecting at this location had pulled off an armed robbery some days previously, so we had to be prepared for a possible shoot-out if things went wrong. But as I sat there trying to snatch a quick five minutes shut-eye after only three hours sleep the day before, my mind played funny tricks on me in that halfway world of nodding off, but still not asleep, one eye open ready to jump into action.

Memories of where it all started just a few years previously crept into my thoughts. I could see in my mind's eye me standing five floors up on the outside of a scaffold surrounding a tower block, in the city of London. I was a self-employed bricky foreman with my own gang working for me, chasing the big penny, or the lump, as it was known then. Whilst I was earning very good money for those days, there was something missing in life, but I couldn't put my finger on it – was it excitement, a bit of danger or just plain insecurity, who knows? Some people take forever to find what they're looking for in life, but one sunny day in May 1967, I found what was missing in mine. Whilst having a casual smoke leaning over the guard rail of the scaffold all the way up there, overlooking the city, I watched the ash from my cigarette tumble down the outside of the scaffold and I noticed a young copper, about my age, in the street below. He was in short-sleeve uniform, chatting up two young female tourists, and was he in his element.

Then out of the line of traffic emerged a police car. Blue lights flashing, sirens going, forcing other cars to drive up on the kerb, it roared to a halt and one of the back doors opened for the PC in question to jump in and off they went screaming into the sunset, or rather down Tottenham Court Road with, I should add, my future along with it. Something inside told me this is what I had been looking for.

Later that night I had a long talk with Sue, my wife, who was always there to encourage me in whatever I did. The following day I made a written application to join the Metropolitan Police and waited for a reply.

Chapter 1

A Change of Direction

Not knowing what kind of a reply I was going to get, Sue and I didn't mention my application to join the police to anybody just in case it all went wrong. Unbeknown to me, the police made quite a few background enquiries, including unannounced visits to my home address to check on my personal circumstances. I should add that by this time Sue and I had moved into a small ground-floor flat in South Woodford, which was the venue of many, many parties. So you can imagine our surprise one Sunday morning some weeks later, at about 9am after one of these parties, when we were awoken by knocking at the front door. 'Who the hell could that be?' I whispered to Sue, as we lay there between the sheets. There followed a frantic scramble and tidy up, which meant chucking everything into the bathroom. This was necessary because it was a very small flat, in fact, the double bed was on a pulley system attached to the wall and the base of the bed, so to change the bedroom into a true 'bedsit' I had to pull the bed up against the wall.

I'd covered the underside of the bed in timber to simulate a fireplace. It looked quite effective, but we were in a mad hurry, and it seemed to take ages. But eventually we were both decent, albeit out of breath. However, as I gently opened the front door, which faced straight onto the street from our lounge, I was greeted by a man dressed very smartly in a suit. My first impression was that he was going to make a complaint about the noise the night before, but no, he just introduced himself as a detective inspector from the local police station.

This was getting worse, I thought, but it appeared he was merely checking on my application to join the force. There he was, standing at my front door surrounded by crates and crates of empty beer bottles and a couple of those red and yellow plastic road cones, which someone had brought to the party the night before. I never realised that police inspectors worked that early on Sunday mornings. Nevertheless, he came in, sat down, then proceeded to put a few questions to both of us, but all the time I'm sure he was aware of our embarrassment. It must have shown on our faces because on leaving you could see a wry smile on his face, as if to say, 'Oh, to be so young and not a care in the world.' That was just it, life was so much fun then – after all, it was the Swinging Sixties!

My decision to try and become a police officer surprised most of my family and friends and devastated others, who had always thought I was one of the 'Chaps', as it was known in certain fraternities. The initial interview in London, some weeks later, seemed to go quite well, and I was informed the following week by way of a very impressive letter that I was to report to Hendon Police Training College in North London on 17 July 1967.

Although at the time I had some second thoughts, I felt I had to give it a go – what had I to lose? In fact, a drop in wages to about a fifth of what I was earning as a foreman bricklayer, but it would mean one small step up the social ladder, and a job more in keeping with what I really wanted in life, a change in direction.

The three months of training at Hendon that followed were traumatic to say the least. First, it was residential and I could only come home at weekends. This proved very difficult to get accustomed to at first, as I had only been married about a year, and was used to home comforts as it were.

I was also used to being in control of my life and when and how I did things, but this was to alter. My attitude towards authority also had to change, bearing in mind I was more at home dealing with fellow building workers as opposed to authoritative figures in uniform. Always having the last word with the instructors was not the wisest thing in the world. This soon became apparent when every time an instructor wanted a volunteer in the practical exercises or a simulated situation it was always, 'We want a volunteer, Woodhouse step forward', which was almost a class joke. Eventually I realised that to think twice and act once was the sensible thing to do, and to keep my mouth shut, which was extremely difficult for a know-it-all, cockney, gobby Jack-the-Lad.

One particular role-play incident that springs to mind was that of a pub-fight situation, set in the college restaurant. The entire class, including me, was gathered outside the closed doors and was told by the class instructor, 'This is the situation, you are on your beat passing a pub and you can hear a lot of noise coming from the supposed pub, i.e. the restaurant, what do you do?' Turning to the class, the instructor continued without drawing breath, 'Volunteer wanted. Thank you Woodhouse.' Naturally, I'd come to expect it and true to form I just stepped forward and dashed in. I think this was the way I generally looked at life, just get stuck in, but on this occasion I was promptly and unceremoniously thrown out again on my backside by at least six strapping drill instructors. Undeterred, I dashed in again for the same thing to happen. After one more try the instructor must have taken pity on me and said, 'Think about this Woody, there must be a better way to go about this.' Then it suddenly dawned on me, 'Shall I call for assistance before I go back in?' This was greeted with, 'Thank God, the penny's dropped.' This was accompanied with lots of laughter from the other members of the class, who, of course, were standing well back within the safety of a crowd where they could hide and didn't have to think on their feet. Taking charge of situations and being in the public eye at the same time was a very new concept for us raw recruits and some found it easier than others.

This cockney know-it-all was gradually transformed into a smart, uniformed, well-trained, knowledgeable, cockney know-it-all police officer.

This was probably the first time in my life I couldn't get away with not studying hard. I found it so difficult to concentrate with the damn dyslexia, and of course the bad spelling didn't help, but I struggled on, thinking it was me. It was no surprise that although I put in an enormous amount of work, I was still only getting average scores at all the written tests, but good marks for all the role plays in taking control of situations. In fact, on one occasion shortly after lunch I was summoned to see the Commandant of the school. I was marched into his very large and impressive office by my class instructor and ordered to stand to attention, whereupon I was asked to resign because I was in the bottom 30 per cent of the class.

I was devastated as I had made such an effort and secretly I was beginning actually to enjoy the hard work. I wasn't going to give in now without a fight, so I just replied, 'No, Sir, you'll have to throw me out.'

'That's the spirit, lad, carry on,' came the reply from a smiling and rather overweight Commandant. I was then quickly marched out of his office. I couldn't believe it, the whole thing was all a set up to see how we recruits would react under stress and pressure, all part of the training, very clever I thought. Well, that wasn't the only thought that crossed my mind as I left that office, perhaps the marriage status of the parents of the Commandant came into question. But there were a couple of lads in the class who just caved in and resigned, not knowing it was a test.

But looking back, of course, they were training us to think on our feet. Life isn't always straightforward. In fact, it rarely is.

Mind you, I did get my own back on a few occasions with the instructors, who on the face of it appeared very strict disciplinarians, hard-faced, no-nonsense guys. So one morning, prior to going on parade, I secreted a small roll of white cotton thread in my top breast pocket with one end protruding down over my dark-blue uniform, just enough for the instructor to see. The trap was set! There must have been two-hundred or so fellow recruits standing to attention that morning on the parade ground, all immaculately turned out, all in double lines in classes of about twenty.

As our class instructor marched by on his final morning inspection, before the main parade began, he obviously noticed something, and stopped right in front of me. He leaned forward and picked the white thread hanging down from my breast pocket and said, 'What have we here, Woodhouse, getting sloppy?', but, of course, as he pulled the thread it just kept coming and coming. After about 3–4ft of thread was unfurled the penny dropped and the whole class burst out in laughter, including the instructor. Well, for a couple of seconds, then he reverted back to his usual shouting, bullying mode, and, of course, an early morning punishment was then dished out, a 6am start picking up cigarette ends. However, it was all worth it, and no doubt the name of the cockney copper was passed round all the other instructors so they could keep an eye on me. It did cross my mind that perhaps it wasn't such a good idea after all.

In a strange way, I must say I did enjoy the three months I spent at Hendon Police College, and although I found it very hard work, I made a few good friends there. It was a place to bring out the more reserved lads and give them self-confidence and bring down to earth the lads like myself who may have been a bit too headstrong, whilst at the same time giving us all the tools and knowledge to do the job on the streets.

On the odd occasion a couple of us would climb over the rear fence at the end of a long day and go for a pint or two in the local pub. In those days the students weren't allowed out of the college grounds in the evening, and, of course, getting back over the fence later on in our condition wasn't quite so easy. In fact, one night, whilst returning from the pub, a mate and I managed to scale the fence alright. However, when I got into the darkened dormitory, or sleeping hut, it was pitch black and I couldn't put the lights on because it would wake everybody up. I just felt my way down the line of beds until I reached my one, except my bed wasn't there, which I couldn't understand. Mine was the eighth one down from the door, nevertheless it wasn't there and there was just a large space. Bearing in mind I'd had a couple of drinks, it all made for a very confusing couple of minutes. I even counted up from the other end of the hut, but there was still a large gap between beds nine and seven. As a result, I just fell asleep in the space on the floor. The next morning I found out why my bed was missing. Whilst I was out at the pub, some of the other lads, who had stayed behind to do some extra studying in the hut, had lifted my bed up into the exposed rafters, fully made up. No wonder I couldn't find it in the dark. Luckily, there wasn't an early morning hut inspection that day as I dread to think of the consequences.

There were other aspects of police training that I found quite difficult to master, things that I hadn't come across before, for example, trying to keep in step whilst marching on the parade ground. About turn was easy, but it only took one plonker to turn the wrong way and it caused complete chaos amongst a squad of twenty officers. How I recall the words 'Woodhouse, how many left feet have you got?' come billowing across the parade ground courtesy of one or other of the drill instructors, on more than one occasion.

But eventually, after so many weeks of hard work, both in and out of the classroom, came the passing out parade. I can honestly say I've never felt so proud in my life of my personal achievements in overcoming all the academic difficulties I had faced during my training and still nobody, including myself, knew why I had found it so challenging. I had yet to discover the word and meaning of 'dyslexia'.

It was a great day, especially for my parents who were so proud to see their son improving himself, albeit within the judicial system rather than in a different direction. This was true of Sue's parents too, who were quite a few rungs further up the social ladder than I was used to, and could now say that their son-in-law was indeed within the law! A police officer had much more standing in society than a mere bricky, not that I did it for them. I merely wanted a bit more excitement and direction in life.

Standing there on parade on that sunny October morning in 1967 amongst dozens and dozens of fellow officers and in front of friends and relatives made all the hard work that we had gone through over the past three months worthwhile. I remember thinking at the time that life was about to kick-start in a new direction, and I couldn't wait to take it on.

Chapter 2

Now the Real Thing

The next eighteen months were spent in Leytonstone, a fairly working class area in the East End of London. This was the birthplace of a number of famous names, including Alfred Hitchcock, the film maker, and David Beckham, the footballer, and one infamous person passed through, reputedly staying at the Green Man pub (now O'Neill's) at the north end at the border with Wanstead. He was Essex born and bred, the highwayman Dick Turpin. He was en route to Norwich, on his trusted Black Bess and eventually his appointment with the hangman at York in 1739. Although a bit before my time, this seemed as good place as any to start my new career within the Metropolitan Police Force, as it was known then.

During the next few weeks I gained valuable experience in dealing with people and situations. For instance, never rush into a pub during a fight amongst a dozen or so market traders, on your own and shout at the top of your voice, 'You're all under arrest'. Does this ring a bell? I remembered too, but not as quickly as I should have done, in fact, I think a little late! However, I soon returned to work after a short period of sick leave a little wiser. Following this episode, together with more and more experience, some of it more unexpected than the rest, I began to increase my knowledge of practical police work, unlike the first time I came across a dead body.

I recall it was a fairly overcast day in October when, whilst out on my beat, about midday I think, I got a message on my radio to go to a small terraced house at the top end of Leytonstone, where a neighbour hadn't seen an old man for some days. On my arrival at the little two-up, two-down semi, I

found the house locked, so I went round the back with the old
lady who had called the police, and found that locked as well. I
couldn't just leave it at that so I forced the back door with my
shoulder, pretending to smell gas, see? Initiative was beginning
to show already. I went inside with the neighbour, but nothing
seemed to be out of order except a rather unpleasant smell,
which appeared to come from upstairs. Putting my handkerchief
over my mouth, I went upstairs and found an old chap in the
front bedroom. He had sadly passed away in bed, but true to my
training I immediately notified my sergeant back at the station
via my radio. I was instructed to search the house for any kind of
correspondence to trace any possible relatives, whilst he notified
the police surgeon to confirm the death and the Coroner's
Officer, who would attend the house in due course.

I should add at this point that the old chap was sitting bolt
upright in the bed, in the corner of the room, leaning against the
walls with his eyes open as if he was watching over his
belongings, very spooky. Nevertheless, I started to look though
his chest of drawers in the bedroom, but all the time I was aware
of his eyes on the back of my neck. Suddenly, without warning,
he must have slumped forward, possibly as a result of the
circulation of air from the door I had left open, which could have
been enough to gently ease the position of his body. As he sank
forwards, the movement forced air out of his body, but all I heard
was this groan from someone or something behind me.

Well, I was out of that house in two seconds flat, scaling the
stairs three or four at a time and screaming like an adolescent
schoolgirl. I found myself standing in the street trembling,
shouting into my radio, 'Serge, he moved and spoke to me!' 'Pull
yourself together, he's been dead for a week', came the reply
from the old sergeant back at the station, and, of course, in the
background I could hear roars of laughter from all the old sweats
in the control room. It took some weeks for that particular story
to die down, mind you it didn't help when some of the lads at
the station would occasionally groan in a deep voice behind my
back, 'I am watching you'.

There then followed a somewhat quite period for a couple of
weeks, until I backed the police van into one of the panda cars

in the police station yard, and transformed the saloon into a hatchback in two seconds. Remember those Morris Minor cars with the light-blue painted doors? They never did make a hatchback, apart from the one I customised!

And then of course there was my first drunk arrest. I think it was late Saturday afternoon when the sergeant called me over from the canteen after my tea break and said, 'Go and arrest that drunk across the road from the nick.' I didn't need telling twice, I dashed out into the street to find a very large lady in her mid-fifties, very scruffy and stinking of booze lying prostrate, full length on the pavement on the other side of the road. As soon as I reached her and knelt down beside her, just to check she was alive, she started shouting out the most disgusting language I have ever heard. It was no good trying to shush her, she just shouted even louder. I helped her to her feet and asked her to cross the road to the police station, where a small crowd of onlookers had gathered, watching my every move. That was my first mistake. I should have just escorted her firmly across the road, but I tried to be a gentleman. She wasn't having any of it. In the struggle, she knocked my helmet off, which went rolling down the road, then in the melee that followed we both went down in the gutter, arms and legs going every where, and, of course, exposing most of her knee-length, grubby, grey knickers to the whole world.

At this point I looked up and saw all the windows of the nick overlooking the street full of faces in rapturous laughter. It appeared she was a regular and always put up a bit of a fight, especially with very young-looking probationer PCs. I eventually got her inside the nick and in a cell for her own safety. Luckily, my police helmet was retrieved from the gutter by a passing old-age pensioner. By today's standards it would probably be pride of place in someone's trophy cabinet along with a couple of road signs – how times have changed.

I was beginning to be known around the area by my colleagues, but not always for the right reasons. The mere mention of my name seemed to bring a knowing smile to the faces of the more experienced officers, as if to say, 'What has he been up to now?' Although I look back with some amusement, at the time I was quite concerned that there was so much to learn because every situation was so different; the classrooms of Hendon seemed a million miles away from the streets of East London in the late sixties.

Then suddenly I had left the sixties and was back in the van and wide awake amongst the other lads on the Flying Squad. The real world had burst back into life with an almighty bang, as if a bomb had gone off just above our heads. The van shook as all the lads braced themselves, only to discover my loaded gun had fallen from my coat pocket onto the metal floor of the vehicle with a resounding clatter as I slumped forward, having nodded off for a split second. Quickly, I regained my presence of mind and murmered, 'Shit, my foot slipped', as if to excuse the unforgivable act of dropping a loaded gun. 'For f**k's sake, Woody,' one of the lads said, 'you could have blown someone's head off with that.' An uneasy silence soon returned as we all settled down in the back of the van once more and I regained my composure. Then, 'I'm bursting for a piss' came from the front of the van, which brought a wry smile to most of the faces sitting in the back, as we had all been there before. The customary large plastic bottle was passed down to the guy at the front, as we all waited for the expected hissing noise of running water. 'Ah, that's better' came from the same direction. 'Alright lads settle down' came from the governor, who was seated in the front. Peace and quiet returned to the little band of brothers huddled in the back of the van, parked in a quiet north London street. Once again, slowly but surely, I slipped into the secure and safe world of memory land, and back to my uniform days on the streets of the East End of London, when I thought perhaps one day I might even make a real copper and eventually write my memoirs, which might begin with the words . . .

Whilst walking my beat as a young copper one bright, sunny Saturday afternoon, well more like strutting in my newly pressed uniform, I came across two Irish gentlemen, well the worst for drink outside a local pub in Leytonstone High Street. They were in loud conversation with each other, and I could just detect a little bit of pushing and shoving, almost to the point where a possible brawl was about to break out.

Hoping to defuse the situation, I strolled up and said something like, 'Alright lads, this is not going to turn nasty is it?' It wasn't until this point that I realised that these two guys stood at least a foot taller than me, even with my police helmet on. What had I got myself into? There was a large intake of breath as I braced myself for what was coming my way. Luckily, one of them gently tapped me on the top of my helmet with his finger and said in a very strong Irish accent, 'It's alright, sir, we don't hit little English policeman' then turned and they put their arms round each others shoulders and walked, well staggered away, struggling to support each other as they made their way down the road. At last, I thought, I was getting the hang of this police lark.

Unbeknown to me, across the road were two older and more experienced police officers standing well back in a doorway. Out of harm's way, they had been watching the whole incident, no doubt waiting for me to succumb to a severe beating at the hands of the two drunks and to see how I handled myself. However, my charm, or more likely my size, or the lack of it, had won the day. Nevertheless, the whole incident was all round the station by the time I had got back for my tea break later that afternoon. Thankfully, the 'little English policeman' nickname only lasted for about a week or two, except for one particular uniformed officer. A couple of years older than me, he, even to this day, some forty-five years later when we occasionally meet in the bar at the local police club in Chigwell, reminds me of this story at every opportunity.

Walking the beat on a lovely sunny day in Leytonstone was priceless in those days. There was respect for the law and the uniformed bobby, to a large extent. At that point in my career I had not come across serious or organised crime. That was to follow sometime in the future, but sometimes the image of pleasant suburbia was somewhat dented.

Let me explain. The commencement of the dreaded double-yellow lines scheme on main roads was a nightmare to all residents, delivery men and, of course, the building and repair trades. I was always more sympathetic to those members of the driving community if I came across them parked on the doubles.

One morning whilst on my beat I noticed a small, open-back lorry parked on double-yellow lines outside a house in Leytonstone High Road. Obviously, the house was having some roof work done, judging by the ladders leading all the way up to the roof. I thought I wouldn't give the driver a ticket, but I had to get the vehicle moved otherwise within minutes half a dozen other vehicles would have parked behind it in the main road. Diligently, I looked around for the driver with no success, apart from a lone figure some four or five floors up on the roof of this particular house.

I shouted up, 'Is this your lorry?' 'What?' came the reply. He appeared to put his cupped hand round his ear and this fiasco was repeated two or three times, then I indicated to him to come down from the roof as I had a sneaky suspicion he was trying to pull a fast one by pretending not to hear what I was saying. He seemed to take forever to climb down the ladders. All part of the game, I thought, but as he got closer to the ground I noticed he had one of his legs heavily strapped up and it was obviously causing him a lot of discomfort. Eventually, he reached the pavement where I started to explain that although I understood his problem with parking the lorry outside the house where he was working, he would still have to move it.

At this point he went absolutely ballistic and explained in no uncertain terms that not only he wouldn't but couldn't move the lorry. 'Why?' I asked. 'Because it's not my f*****g lorry and don't know who it belongs to.'

My apologies did not seem to be accepted as he told me to 'F**k off' in no uncertain terms as he started to climb up the ladder again. This, I thought at the time, was good advice, bearing in mind this chap's size and demeanour, so that's exactly what I did, leaving the lorry sticking out like a sore thumb on the two double-yellow lines in the High Road. I think this lesson is called one of expedience. Never start trouble unless you can finish it.

It wasn't long before the bitter winter of 1967/68 arrived, but now I didn't have to handle icy bricks on a building site, stuck together, ripping my fingers to shreds every time I picked one up and then wincing in pain as it slipped through my fingers taking some of the skin with it. My new situation, therefore, was a vast improvement.

Although the early turn at the station started at 5.45am, it was not as bad as I first thought. In fact, it was quite busy because of the rush hour, which lasted until at least 9am with all that entailed with traffic congestion, then all the overnight crime reports that came in to the station, such as burglaries that the night duty had missed, as well as car thefts and criminal damage. Then came breakfast, a welcome break, cooking your own food on a small one-ring burner in the corner of the canteen, which was originally the police horse stables. Updated, of course, just. That was the norm back then, refreshments were very much a DIY affair.

I recall strolling down the street on many occasions to the local bakers-cum-coffee shop, about mid-morning. It was only a couple of hundred yards down from Leytonstone nick. Usually, I would purchase two fresh rolls from the baker's and a quarter of a pound of sausage meat from the butcher's next door, which I pushed up into the top of my police helmet, then forcing it down on top of my head, to the great amusement of the staff in the baker's shop. It was alright balancing my helmet on top of my head provided I didn't have to run or turn my head quickly. I must have looked like one of those young girls at finishing school trying to walk upright with a couple of books balanced on their heads to improve deportment. It wasn't done in those days for a uniformed PC to be seen walking the streets with a shopping bag of food in his hands, hence the subterfuge. Anyhow, two freshly cooked burgers in newly baked rolls were enough to keep anybody going for a few hours.

After breakfast one particular bitter snowy and icy morning my casual walk took me down to Harrow Road, about a quarter of a mile from Leytonstone nick, where I found a long line of cars stationary in the snow on both sides of a steep incline. It had become very icy due to cars spinning their wheels too fast as they attempted to gain traction in order to reach the other side of the hill.

It was time to use some 'out of the box' thinking. Having just come from the building sites of London a few months earlier, I was well acquainted with the uneasiness that building workers had with the idea of police on their sites, and would do anything to help just to get rid of a uniformed bobby.

So, on seeing a large building site nearby I thought I could turn this to my advantage, and marched into the general foreman's office expecting a somewhat frosty reception. However, to my surprise I was greeted by a gent of the old school who was old enough to be my granddad. He came out with a most unexpected opening line, 'And what can I do for you officer?' I explained that a until few months previously I had been working in the building trade on sites much like this one, but had changed my career, so we had something in common. There followed a short conversation over a cup of building site tea, served up in the usual dirty china mug, which had not seen hot, soapy water for many months. I pointed out the road situation just outside the gates of his site. 'Well,' said my new-found friend, 'we can't have that can we officer, follow me'. As we reached the door of his office I noticed a small group of workers gathering in the cold just yards away. They had obviously been told of my presence via the grapevine, and were quietly waiting, no doubt, for one of their number to be marched off to the nick for some small infringement of the law. So, it was with great relief on their part when they discovered that all I wanted was a bit of gritty sand. They all manually filled a dumper truck full of sharp sand and drove it to the main entrance within a couple of minutes, where I climbed aboard to shouts of 'Wagons ho!' There I was, standing on the back of a bright-yellow dumper truck, in full uniform, leading a small army of labourers to the base of the ice-covered hill to the applause of all the stranded car drivers. Needless to say, within minutes the sand was spread on the road and cars were on the move.

With a little bit of self-satisfaction I strolled off back to the station, where I recounted the greatly enhanced story of my initiative to my sergeant. It was greeted unsympathetically with the words, 'Let's hope we don't get a bill for 5 ton of sand.' I was devastated, not only by the lack encouragement shown by the sergeant but by the thought of the possible payment for 5 ton of sand, which had not crossed my mind. Oh dear! Happily, I was spared that embarrassment.

A week later I was on night duty, and it was even colder, but I didn't mind. I found it strangely exciting creeping around the backs of shops and offices at two or three in the morning looking for, and more importantly listening out for, the sound of suspects breaking glass or muffled voices of burglars working in the dead of night.

Unfortunately, after many nights patrolling the streets, I realised it wasn't that easy to catch burglars in the act. So, I decided not to be so enthusiastic, by going about my duties like a lion in the undergrowth of the African Serengeti, seeking out its prey, but to take a more laid-back approach. If I came across it, all well and good, but I would concentrate more on just observing things around me, rather like an owl, whilst on my nocturnal walkabouts.

The following night I was again walking behind the shops in Leytonstone High Road on my way back to the station for my 4am cup of tea, when I noticed an alleyway about 4ft wide leading from the back of the row of shops straight onto the High Road. The buildings on the first floor, however, joined over the top to form a tunnel.

Now, bearing in mind the low, sub-zero temperatures that night and the obliging leaking drainpipe at the rear entrance to the alleyway, a sheet of ice had formed at least 2in thick along the full length of the alley and extended out onto the pavement of the High Road. 'Well, why not?' I thought, nobody's about and here is a chance to break the monotony of night duty. So, after taking a long run up, I jumped onto the end of the ice slide and promptly stood bolt upright to attention as I glided down the alleyway. Absolutely marvellous, a kind of lateral bungee jumping. I popped out onto the High Road still standing to attention rather like those clocks that have two figures that come out when forecasting rain or fine weather.

On reaching the end of the slide I just stepped off smartly and carried on casually walking, when at this point I noticed an old lady just yards away, who was obviously an early morning cleaner on her way to work. The look on her face was priceless as I walked passed the startled women and said, 'Morning, madam' in a true 1940s 'Dixon of Dock Green' fashion. What must have gone through her mind, perhaps a future Flying Squad officer in the making, no surely not, more like a little boy completely oblivious to the world around him, just having fun.

As a young police officer I learned very quickly there is no substitute for experience, which is gained by hard work, persistence and, of course, a little luck. I've always had a knack of tripping over luck, rather than finding it in a blaze of glory; let me explain.

Whilst on one of my early stints of night duty, in a panda car, I came across a young guy in his twenties walking down one of the back streets of Leytonstone in the early hours carrying a holdall. Nothing wrong with that you may say, but I just wanted a chat to pass the time, so I stopped him. 'Just off to work then?' I asked. 'Yes,' he replied. 'What's in the bag?' I enquired. 'Oh, just my tools' came the reply, then, with one almighty blow with the bag, I was on my back and this guy was running down the road like a scalded cat.

Undeterred but a little dazed, I jumped to my feet and was after him, leaving the bag and its contents lying all over the pavement by the swinging door of my abandoned panda car.

There I was in the middle of the night, completely on my own, in hot pursuit of this dastardly violent criminal, and who knows he may well have been armed, just because I wanted a chat to pass the time. Obviously, I must have upset him in some way.

It's a funny thing when you think you are all alone, you rarely are. Unbeknown to me, this whole incident was being watched by an old lady in an upstairs window across the road. She obviously couldn't sleep that night for some reason and decided to gaze into the night sky. Anyhow, she saved my bacon that night, by ringing 999 at Scotland Yard, who in turn informed all the local patrol cars in the area to search for me and my violent suspect.

Meanwhile, I was still running up and down the back streets of Leytonstone after my attacker. There came a point, however, when I couldn't run any more, I had run my heart out and I was exhausted, knackered, fit to drop. Suddenly, the guy I was chasing dropped to the ground and shouted, 'Alright, that's it, I can't run another step.' Little did he know I had already stopped one second earlier, and I soon had him marching down the road, with his arm up his back, in the direction of my abandoned panda car. Then in the distance I heard the welcome sound of the two-tone horns of police cars, safe in the knowledge that help was at hand. We were soon picked up by one of the cars searching for us, all thanks to the phone call made by the little old lady in the window.

When I got the man back to the station and searched his bag the sergeant and I found it contained about £250 all in shillings, or 5p as it is now. During the next hour of interrogation it transpired he was from the Midlands and had broken into a workingman's club near Manchester earlier that night and taken the coins from all the slot machines. He had then stolen a car and driven down to London, and had just run out of petrol round the corner from where I encountered him. Having been unable to find a petrol station open, he was out looking for another car to steal just minutes before I had stopped him. He later said he would never come to London again because the police were far too good. If only he'd known all I wanted was a chat to pass the time in the middle of the night on a boring duty. If I remember correctly, he got three months for his trouble, and I got a slap on the back for a job well done from the sergeant.

There were the odd occasions when violence did raise its ugly head, but by and large the streets of Leytonstone were fairly safe. I experienced more dangerous scenarios whilst assisting in crowd control (or riot duty) up in London together with hundreds of other officers from all over the Met. Now, no matter how well organised, occasionally some times small units of officers get cut off from the main body of police and become vulnerable during a riot, and that's just what happened to me. Somehow four of us found ourselves standing in front of a 12ft-tall glass shop window just off the Strand, and in front of us was a very large angry crowd, of well over a hundred, and they were heading straight for us. One of the more experienced PCs with me shouted, 'Draw your truncheons, lads, I think we've got a bit of a problem.' He wasn't far wrong. With this large glass window behind us there was nowhere for us to go, and we just had to stand and fight or be thrown back into the window by the protesters, with disastrous consequences.

This was the first time in my adult life that I felt a warm trickle running down the inside of my leg. 'Scared' doesn't really describe the feeling enough. Petrified would be more accurate, but with seconds to spare we were joined by a dozen or so officers who had just turned the corner. The feeling of relief was breathtaking, and, needless to say, with our numbers swelled the rioters backed off and left us alone. A few hours later when I was relating this story to some of the other PCs on the coach on the way back to Leytonstone, it had become more akin to the scene from the film *Zulu* in which Michael Caine faces thousands of Zulus at Rorke's Drift. Obviously, the story got better by the telling, and by then the inside of my trousers had completely dried off and had been omitted from my memory, until now.

A couple of weeks after this incident, I was ordered to attend one of the nearby divisions by one of the best exponents of the art of interrogation I have ever met. Some say he was a slightly eccentric detective inspector, but to me, back then in those days, I considered him to be just on the right-hand side of God. This opinion was held by most of us lowly uniformed officers, and also by many of the CID officers under him at the time, a view I still hold today. Sadly, he has now passed on and will no doubt appear before the great judge in the sky to receive a richly deserved commendation for his outstanding work in helping to put a large number of villains behind bars and out of harm's way.

He had called me over regarding an allegation of theft during a recent protest I had attended up town that had been allocated to him to investigate. For a very young and naive uniformed officer to be interviewed by a detective inspector with his rank and reputation was like being called to stand trial at the Old Bailey – a really awesome situation!

So, when I arrived at the CID office at the allotted time you can imagine I felt quite intimidated. George, as I shall call him, could obviously see how nervous I was. But he sat me down and asked if I was aware of a protester losing his watch at a recent demonstration up town that I had attended on duty. A well-known protester, known for making frequent complaints, had obviously made a false allegation of theft of his watch, which I doubt existed in the first place, to claim compensation and to cause aggravation to the police. This was apparently complete news to me, and it evidently showed on my face. He then said, 'Mister,' a term he often used, 'Look, Learn and Remember', and then proceeded to interview me and take a statement without actually putting words into my mouth and then asked me to sign the statement. I felt so grateful for this lesson in true interrogation skills on how to obtain information without thumping the table but by more subtle methods, by using well-mannered, pertinent questioning delivered in normal tones to obtain intelligence directed to a very young officer, who was totally out of his depth.

However, a few years later, as I got to know him better as a junior detective, I was fined numerous bottles of Scotch over a long period of time along with other officers (which would be used for the Friday-night office get-together) for any 'slight administrating indiscretions', another term he was fond of using. I considered this fair payment for services received in my early career as a detective. I recall with great fondness the words, 'Ah, that will cost you a bottle, Mister' directed to some other unfortunate young CID officer, late on most Friday evenings. The man was not only a fantastic thief-taker, but a real character, unfortunately now a dying breed.

Now, some would say this is an ideal time to relate this next story, but you will have to be the judge. It was the talk of many east London police stations for a number of months.

It involved a very senior officer, who shall remain nameless because he was the most despicable and hated man I have ever had the misfortune to meet. On one occasion I was directed to a neighbouring division to be his temporary driver. I spent the day being barked at every couple of minutes between a number of local police stations until lunchtime. Then I was ordered to convey him to and from a number of local pubs, where he became more and more intoxicated. By about 11pm he could hardly stand, but he could still shout, ordering me to drive him home. On reaching his home address, I opened the rear car door to see him literally fall out at my feet – he was helpless, unable to speak, sprawled over the pavement outside his house, unable to get to his feet, so I just left him there and drove back to the station, without saying a word to anyone. It was no more than he deserved.

Anyhow, back to the main story concerning this very senior officer, who it appears was about to retire. This officer was, for some reason, delivering a hell of a dressing down to a, let's say, middle-ranking officer, junior to him, in his office on the top floor of a police station somewhere in east London. The recipient of this admonishment, I think his name was George, had obviously had enough of his abuse over the years so he just stood there in front of his desk, undid his trouser flies and urinated all over this very senior officer's desk as he sat there shouting.

Having made his feelings felt in this very expressive manor, he turned and left the office, saying to all who had now gathered in the corridor as a result of the shouting, 'He's lost it, he's finally gone mad, you better ring for the men in white coats' as he disappeared down the stairs to his office to grab his coat and no doubt get an early night.

Chapter 3

Back to Reality

uddenly, I had this strange feeling of being in a burning house, it seemed so real and intense as I spluttered and coughed, then I realised that Mick, a 6ft DC whose favourite sport was rugby when sober and bare knuckle fighting in pubs when pissed, was sitting opposite me in the van. He was blowing smoke rings in my direction, but although this was slightly irritating he was a great guy to have on your side when in trouble and being a smoker myself it wasn't really a problem.

However, it did bring me back to reality and the job in hand, armed robbers, who were due to cross our path very shortly. It appeared that on this occasion one of the lads on my team, on the Flying Squad, had been contacted by one of his informants with information concerning a robbery that had taken place in London the week before. He said the gang involved were holed up in a flat in north London, and were waiting for the arrival of a 'fence' (one who receives stolen goods) to come and take the proceeds of the crime and pay them out in clean money. Now, because it could prove very dangerous to take the villains inside a building, it was decided to get them out into the street, hopefully in a quiet area, and take them down without any shots being fired. So, the informant arranged for the gang to meet the 'fence' (and no prizes for guessing who he was) at a location half a mile away from their flat, which meant the gang had to travel to this new location by way of one particular one-way street.

So, we had the time and the route the gang would be travelling, the place and the fire power, plus the informant to set the meet up. The villains didn't really stand a chance, and why should they – they were the men who the previous week had robbed two security guards at gun point, and threatened to shoot them between the legs if they offered any resistance! These were the type of men we were dealing with, so-called 'hard men'. Well, it was our turn to show them who the real men were.

On this cold, miserable morning in early 1978 in north London at about 11am the team was in position, on both sides of this road, hidden away by bushes and unoccupied buildings. This was also an ideal location for our nondescript vans, with no people about to get hurt if any thing went wrong and shots were fired. It was my job to dash out in front of the van, some 10–20yd away, draw my 38 Smith and Western revolver and take a shooting stance in the middle of the road. This would hopefully force the van to a stop, whilst other officers would simultaneously attack the van from both sides, opening the doors and dragging the occupants out, all in the matter of seconds. All went well and the van arrived, with three occupants, on time. I jumped out and took my position, as arranged, and shouted 'Stop! Armed police!' which seemed to do the trick and, thank God, the van screamed to a halt. Then the other lads hit the villains from both sides, opening the doors and dragging the occupants out onto the street before they had time to think.

After they had been pulled out of the van they were bundled against the wall in the spread-eagle position within seconds, guns pointed at them from all directions, whilst they were rubbed down and searched for any weapons. We found two hand guns and a sawn-off shotgun on them. Meanwhile, I was still in my position in the middle of the road, with my gun trained on the van, when the detective inspector shouted, 'For f**k's sake, Woody', or words to that effect, 'put that effing gun away, you're liable to hurt someone.' Obviously, he didn't think much of my newly acquired firearms technique. One thing I did notice as I approached the villains, as I replaced my gun in my shoulder holster, was that they were still standing, with their hands in the air against the wall, and without exception all three men had pissed themselves. In fact, one had gone even further, so much for 'hard men'. No more the swagger, especially when they were handcuffed and bundled into the back of a waiting police van.

Later that day, all three where interviewed back at the nick, and couldn't talk enough, especially about their fellow robbers' participation in the robbery a few days previously. So much for 'honour amongst thieves'. Funny thing is, although they were given the opportunity a number of times, no mention was made of why they were there at that time and place. Our informant obviously lived to fight another day!

I've never been frightened of firearms but I do have a healthy respect for guns. I say that, but I was once put to the test at a firearms refresher course, which came up roughly every couple of months for authorised firearms officers. There were a dozen other officers from all over east London at this particular course. We were split into three groups of four and took it in turns to shoot from different positions and distances.

On completion of one of these test shoots the officer next to me, who was holding his pistol at shoulder height, suddenly blew down the barrel then swivelled the gun round like an American gunslinger in a Western movie. It suddenly dawned on me that this idiot of a guy could be standing behind me at a firearms incident sometime in the future. What a sobering thought. I understand today in the modern 'police service' that all officers undergo a profile assessment before training as a firearms officer to weed out fools like the above, thank God.

It was a great feeling being on the Flying Squad surrounded by good-quality thief-takers, but my next experience was a bit hairy. One of the lads on the team had got quite close to a gang that was stealing lorries and their loads in another part of London and bringing them to the outskirts of east London, where they were selling the goods. Now being fairly new on the Squad and on the small side in comparison to the majority of the lads, I didn't really look like a copper, especially as I wore thick, black, horn-rimmed Michael Caine glasses, which was quite unusual for a copper in those days,

I suppose I was the obvious choice, so I was briefed to turn up, a few nights later, at about 10pm near a farm track leading from the main A127 road, near Romford in Essex, and attempt to buy one of these lorry loads. Whilst the rest of the team was to be secreted nearby, arrangements where made for me to be wired up with a microphone so my colleagues would know what was going on at all times.

It's not something anyone can teach you, but buying stolen goods can be very difficult. If the thieves think at any time that you're not the real thing, and that the police are involved, they will just make a run for it after giving you a bloody good hiding. This is why the stolen lorry and its load are hidden away until a price has been agreed, then, and only then, do the villains produce the lorry for inspection. If the price is too low, you lose the load, too high you give the game away as being a possible set-up. Eventually, I managed to agree a price, but stalled the thieves by not showing them the money until I could inspect the goods. I then waited for the lorry to turn up, whilst still in the company of the villains, who were watching my every move like a hawk and sussing me out.

Now, on this particular night our team was a bit short of lads so the guv'nor (detective inspector) had arranged for some uniformed lads from the local nick to help us out and cover the outer ring surrounding the meeting place. So, the scene was set, all ready for me to say a certain code word into my microphone when I saw the lorry arrive. This was the signal to close in and arrest the lorry thieves and recover the stolen lorry and goods. It was also necessary for me to make good my escape from the scene, and not to be captured by police in order not to complicate the situation when eventually we arrived in court some months later. We didn't want the villain to guess where the information came from and it was far easier not to get involved with 'agent provocateur'! In this case, the theft had already taken place, so police were merely recovering stolen goods as a result of information. It was much more straightforward this way and it took the dairy away from the informant. (Dairy farm – harm – cockney rhyming slang.)

When I saw the lorry coming up the farm track towards us, I gave the signal for police to move in, and I started to make good my escape, or in other words, get the hell out of there as quick as possible before I had my nuts blown off by the villains who may have guessed they had been set up. I jumped over a nearby fence and ran across a large, open field towards some houses, leaving the villains to their fate. Unfortunately, coming from the other direction I could just make out, by way of the street lights on the main road, a figure with a shiny badge on the front of his helmet. He was heading in my direction, so I ducked down and made my way over to the rear of the houses and climbed a fence into a back garden. Looking back, I could see the helmet still coming in my direction. I managed to climb up onto the roof of a shed to hide. There I lay for what seemed forever, my heart pounding, whilst trying to get my breath back, having just run across an open field. Suddenly, a head popped up over the shed roof, and the uniformed copper had found me. He then made a grab for my leg, instinctively I kicked out in an attempt to release his grip on me but unfortunately hit the officer squarely in the face. I didn't mean to hurt him but I had to get away. I heard the officer grunt and fall back down to the ground, amongst a load of bushes, which allowed time for me to jump down on the other side of the fence into another garden and run down the side and away into the night and make good my escape.

I had to keep well out of the way the rest of that night in case I was recognised by any of the villains in the vicinity who may have got away from the scene. I recall going to a local cinema and sitting in the dark for a couple of hours watching some Western whilst keeping an eye out for latecomers to the film who may have looked familiar.

Some days later I arranged for a local CID officer to deliver a compensatory bottle of Scotch to the home address of the PC I had encountered on the shed roof. The officer apologised on my behalf for the slight injury caused and discreetly explained the reason for my actions. Other than that, the operation was a complete success, the gang were all rounded up, plus one stolen lorry and load recovered. Nobody was hurt, except the dignity of one uniformed officer who now, no doubt, often relates the story over a few pints in his local of the time he arrested a whole team of thieves whilst omitting the detail where he was gently kicked in the face by the one that got away.

Shortly afterwards, I think a couple of weeks later, I was posted to a very unfamiliar and strange duty, that of looking after villains, whilst armed with a snub-nosed Smith and Western 38. Yes, the era of the 'supergrass' had arrived! It was called 'protective custody'. There were several different teams, some to interview the villains and to take statements, others to investigate similar offences and to collate it all together. The team I was on was the close protection, accommodation and transporting team. We worked twelve hours on duty, twelve hours off every day for months. Not surprisingly, some of the villains we got to know very well, on first-name terms, but of course you had to be on your guard at all times, watching the slippery buggers and looking out for the villains who were yet to be arrested on their information, who were out to kill our charges for grassing them up. All a bit hairy, I can tell you.

One particular night, my small team was guarding two villains overnight at a small out of the way police station on the outskirts of north London. Just before midnight we had a phone call from the main office at the Yard to the effect that information had been received that indicated that an attack by armed villains was expected that night, at 'a' north London police station to free the supergrasses and then execute them as a warning to others to keep their mouths shut! Looking back it sounded more like a senior officer had made a casual remark to one of his subordinates, to the effect of 'better keep them lads at the outer stations on their toes'.

This obviously prompted some idiot with an over active imagination to make the phone call, but at the time it put the fear of God in us all that night. Come to think of it, there were quite a few visits to loos in the cells that night whilst thinking what might be in store for us during the next few hours, so we were ready for anything all night, up until dawn, which didn't arrive too soon. But I suppose it had the desired effect. I think it also caused more than a little anxiety amongst our protected guests, but of course that goes with the territory. Thinking about it, there were far too many small police stations dotted in and around the London area to be covered by sufficient armed officers, so it was down to us to look after ourselves if there was an attempt to kill our guests.

Mind you, during the next few weeks it was very interesting taking one particular villain to a number of museums and old country houses all over London and the Home Counties as part of the investigation. At these locations he showed us where and how he had forced open glass cabinets and show cases and stolen priceless small items of jewellery under the noses of the shaven-headed, 18-stone so-called security staff. These valuable pieces were later sold on at a fraction of their true value. He had been doing this for years, causing priceless items to be passed onto the black market never to see the light of day again, unless they were recovered by pure chance by police intervention.

Nobody who served on the Flying Squad in those day's can even attempt adequately to describe on paper what a thrilling time it was. Political correctness had never been heard of. The courts backed us to the hilt and, usually, just the peremptory shout of 'Squad' was sufficient to bring the villains out, hands held high. The prospect of the next four years of hair-raising white-knuckle car chases, hours of observations outside banks until the robbers turned up just as the security van arrived and then the exciting dash across the pavement armed with either a pickaxe handle or on some occasions a 38 snub-nose Smith and Western to then jump on a team of unscrupulous criminals who had scant regard for human life and knock the stuffing out of them was exhilarating.

Not all the jobs were violent. In fact, one of my first on the Squad was very straightforward. A call from the Regional Crime Squad, or RCS, up in Aberdeen, with a request to 'turn over a flop' (search an address by way of a warrant) and arrest a man for the robbery of highly valued jewellery, at gun point, in Aberdeen the week previously. It appeared the RCS had found out the address of an ex-girlfriend in London, and thought the robber might be hiding out there.

One of the DSs, who took the call and whom I shall call Bob, a guy I knew back from my Ilford days, said, 'Come on, Woody, a nice easy raid first thing in the morning.'

The next day, shortly before 6am, the two of us, plus a few uniform lads, raided a flat in north London. The door was smashed in so quickly, by the time Bob and I got into his bedroom, the suspect was still rubbing his eyes. I immediately pulled off the bed clothes and jumped straight across the bed to restrain him, not noticing there was another person in the bed with him.

I don't know who was more surprised, the young lady, the suspect or me. It was like a kid's pillow fight, arms and legs everywhere, plus all the shouting and screaming from the girl. One saving grace was that I was the one with my clothes on! Once Bob and I had established what bits of body I had grabbed belonged to whom, we arrested and handcuffed the suspect. Then a search of the room revealed all the jewellery in a case, under the bed, and a gun under the pillow where he had been lying. Luckily, the search was a complete surprise so it was a bit of a shock for the suspect that early in the morning, he didn't have the time to pull himself together and use the gun. Anyway, the prisoner plus all the jewellery and the gun soon found there way to the nearest nick, where he was detained awaiting the arrival of officers from Aberdeen to collect him and take him back to face trial in Scotland.

What normally happens when visiting officers come to the Met from other forces is that they are looked after, and taken out for a night out on the town. I must say at this point that other forces seem to do a far better job of entertaining Met officers then we do. Perhaps we tend to get more visitors than they do.

I remember on this occasion that it was a fairly low-key affair, as the two lads from Aberdeen were shattered because they had come down from Scotland that day by train, so they returned to their hotel quite early that night. The following day they duly collected their prisoner with the stolen property and returned to Scotland. They also took with them two short statements of arrest from Bob and me, which would be read out in court at the prisoner's trial, where, no doubt, he would have pleaded guilty because of the overwhelming evidence against him. A nice little job with no aggravation.

'Ah!' I hear you say, 'Far too easy.' You were right. Some months later a request was received at the Yard from Aberdeen for Bob and me to attend the Sheriffs High Court for the trial of some guy, whose name neither of us could remember, for an armed robbery in Aberdeen. It took some days for us to get to the bottom of it and dig out our original notes, but eventually a week later Bob and I were taken to Stansted Airport by a squad car to catch a flight to Aberdeen.

Unbeknown to me, Bob was just as uneasy about flying as I was, so consequently as soon as we reached our seats in the aircraft and had taken off we were downing gin and tonics as fast as the stewards could bring them. I know the flight is only an hour, but Bob and I were quite happy when we arrived at Aberdeen Airport.

To describe Aberdeen Airport as a quiet provincial airport is quite frankly an understatement. It had an extremely large and spacious concourse, probably due to the considerable amount of traffic to the oil rigs in the area. Anyhow, on this particular day things were fairly quiet. So, when the young uniformed officer sent to collect us arranged for a call on the public-address system to the effect, 'Would the two Scotland Yard officers arriving from London kindly report to the police office, by the main entrance' it was no surprise to see heads turn as Bob and I walked right across the middle of the biggest deserted concourse you have ever seen.

It seemed to take for ever, and every step was watched by hundreds of onlookers seated all round the edge awaiting their flights. Now, remembering both Bob and I had had a good drink, a thought crossed my mind, just for a joke of course, shall I take hold of Bob's hand? On second thoughts I decided against it, thinking he wouldn't have the balls to carry it off, so we carried on with the well-practised macho Squad stroll towards the police office, where we were met by our escort, a young PC who looked about 15 years old.

'This way, Sir,' he said, as he grabbed our bags and placed them in the boot of a fully painted yellow and blue traffic car with all lights flashing – the Commissioner himself wouldn't have commanded more respect. Straight to the hotel at high speed, with all lights flashing, just to drop the bags off, no time to book in. This officer was obviously under strict orders. Again at racing pace we were whisked off to the next venue, which turned out to be a club, somewhere in the centre of Aberdeen. On entering the club, we saw a vast area with a huge high ceiling, more like a dance hall than a drinking club. At first glance it appeared solely occupied by all the officers from the local RCS who had obviously started the party well before our arrival. We were introduced to the Governor, or Boss as they called him, and then pointed in the direction of the bar. The Aberdeen accent is fairly strong at the best of times, but mix in a few pints and it was almost impossible to understand what was being said. We had to rely upon every other word and a bit of sign language accompanied with the occasional nodding of the head, which we blamed on the loud music in the background, but Bob and I muddled through somehow. All in all they made us very welcome.

It was plain to see this was going to be very long, hard night. In fact, shortly after midnight, I clearly remember, well perhaps not too clearly, going to the loo, which was at the top of a long, open staircase attached to the back wall, and in full view of all there. Climbing the stairs was difficult enough, but as I reached the top step I lost my balance, and came crashing down to the bottom in a dishevelled mess. Not much of a party trick, you may say, but I was holding a full glass of gin and tonic at this point. I had just enough time to place my hand over the top of the glass to stop any spillages. On regaining my feet and my composure at the bottom of the staircase, I was subjected to an enormous round of applause for my presence of mind, and dexterity, not having spilt a drop. So, the night went on and on, well into the early hours, when eventually Bob and I were poured into our respective beds, back at the hotel somewhere in the middle of Aberdeen. I remember a lot of running to and fro to the loo, which was a couple of doors up from our room, most of the night.

But, eventually the very unwanted chinks of light forced their way through the curtains of the hotel bedroom, heralding the next day with a bang. God, did I feel bad, my mouth felt like someone or something had slept in it, and by the looks of Bob he was no better. It took an enormous amount of effort to pull ourselves together, just in time to be collected by the RCS and taken to the court.

This was my first time in a Scottish High Court. It was a very splendid affair, with all the coats of arms all round the walls and even the uniform police officers where wearing white gloves. When the judge entered the court, dressed in all his finery and brightly coloured regalia, it was a very impressive sight. All I had to do, when called upon, was read from my police pocket book the facts in the case concerning the arrest of the suspect, back in London, some months prior. However, my hands were shaking so badly I had to hold it with both them, plus there was the uneasy feeling in the stomach region and the recurring question in my mind, would I throw up in the middle of the court? God, all I wanted was to die. Then the suspect was brought into the court and the charge was put to him, 'Guilty' came the reply from the dock, thank Christ, no need to give evidence of his arrest now. I almost stood up and cheered, but I managed to control myself. But then I turned to the Scottish RCS officer sitting by my side, and said, 'Why did you call us up here to give evidence when you must have known he was going to plead guilty?' 'Well, it was a trip out for you both' came the reply, a statement I couldn't really disagree with.

Have you ever heard of the old saying 'the hair of the dog'? Well, Bob and I certainly needed just that, more than life itself. Of course, not having had any food for some time, it didn't take long before we were both quite happy once more. As time marched on during that day, and continued into the evening, still in the company of our hosts, the question of flight times went completely out of our heads. Hence the reason for a further night's stay in the hot spots of Aberdeen. We never did get to see it in daylight.

I remember thinking at about the time I joined the Squad, a few months prior, 'Please, God, help me to avoid any "cock-ups"', and remembering the little prayer about stepping on toes that may be connected to an arse you may have to kiss at a later stage, well you know what I mean. The next few days were a sign of things to come, thirteen to fourteen hours a day was the norm, and on cue my guardian angel looked after me well for a couple of months, then disaster. Let me explain.

Chapter 4

Never Say 'We' When You Mean 'They'

t is not widely known (by today's young coppers, I mean) but thirty years ago, Friday nights at Scotland Yard and CID offices everywhere within the jurisdiction of the Metropolitan Police signalled a cessation of work and the uncorking of bottles of Scotch. The 'Friday night wind-down in the office' had begun. It was a welcome relief after a week of early morning search warrants, late-night observations, court appearances and the never-ending tide of robberies, burglaries, assaults, all of which were accompanied with a mountain of paperwork.

It was a chance to relax, wind down, have a laugh and a joke, discuss work and often iron out differences in the CID office before they got out of control. Nowadays, police officers in similar situations go rushing to militant action groups and get paid out scandalous amounts of money by washing their dirty linen in public and bringing down the reputation of the Force. So you tell me, what's the better way to settle the dust and defuse any disputes? But I digress.

Everybody was expected to attend these gatherings but on this particular Friday night, quite a few months earlier, I, as a fairly new detective constable working at Plaistow Police Station in the East End of London, was expected to contribute not only a bottle of Scotch but also a few cans of beer! Anyhow, there I was chatting with a couple of CID officers when my attention was drawn to a conversation behind me being conducted between a shapely CID office typist and an uninvited uniformed PC who had come out with probably the most cretinous chat-up line I have ever heard.

I heard the PC say to her, 'Well, you know all morris dancers are queer!' What prompted this incredible assertion I've no idea but I decided that this was an opportunity not to be missed. Turning round I gave him 'a look' and said, 'Funny you should say that, I suppose by the law of averages some morris dancers might be queer, but here's one who most definitely ain't.' Dropping his eyes his face flushed, but I was nowhere near finished with him yet, oh dear me no. 'WE go out every Sunday morning,' I continued, 'and apart from the enjoyment and the large amount of cash we earn for charity, we're keeping alive the historic values and traditions of English country dancing. Can you say the same?' The look on that young uniformed copper's face, as he slouched off was reward itself. Then from the side of me came this very young and attractive female voice, 'I didn't know you were a morris dancer,' said the typist quietly. 'There's more to you than meets the eye.' Steady lad! Pull your self together, I thought!

All I had wanted to do was to put down a jumped up little twerp too big for his boots, who was trying to impress the CID typist in our office. How was I to know that I'd started the ball rolling on something that was to become the topic of many conversations throughout the Metropolitan Police over the next twenty years and would almost succeed in getting me kicked back to uniform? The mistake was simple, all I'd said was 'WE' instead of 'THEY' go out every Sunday morning.

None of this was immediately apparent, of course. Mind you, I must have been fairly convincing, as over the next hour or two I received many requests for me and my – imaginary – dance troupe to attend local school fetes, charity events and several worthwhile fundraisers from my fellow colleagues. To all such requests, I explained the story was just a joke, and I only said it to put down the PC, adding that I knew as much about old English folklore as I did about childbirth. Over the next few weeks and months the story died down and was finally laid to rest, or so I thought, until my new posting to New Scotland Yard.

I was propelled into the rough, tough world of *The Sweeney*, the elite and world-famous Flying Squad at New Scotland Yard, which ever since its inception in 1919 has been a byword for toughness through the unorthodox ways it deals with professional and hardened criminals. On my arrival on the Squad, a couple of months before Christmas, I was posted to 'One Squad', where shortly afterwards I was told to attend a full Flying Squad social club meeting called at the Yard. All twelve squads, each of them containing about a dozen or so of the most experienced thief-takers in the Metropolitan Police, attended.

It transpired that every year the Squad organised a stag night at Quaglino's, a very prestigious London nightspot, for which everyone attended in evening suits. All twelve squads were expected to provide some entertainment by doing a sketch, a song or some sort of party piece. Wow! I thought – this sounds terrific fun; I couldn't wait to get involved. Following the main meeting, our Detective Inspector, Tony Stevens, called a much smaller meeting of our own One Squad. He said, 'Right, listen up, lads' as he leaned forward in a conspiratorial sort of way. 'Last year, our team put on the best act. It put all the others in the shade, remember?' There were nods of agreement and grunts of 'too right!' 'And this year, it's going to be no exception because we've got Woody here, our new team member', and as he gestured in my direction, my chest swelled up and I felt I grew a foot taller.

Here I was, the new boy on the block and already a bloody star! The detective inspector continued, 'And because Woody is a very experienced morris dancer,' and here he paused, due to the roars of laughter sweeping the office, 'we'll be dressing up as a troupe of morris dancers with bells, the full authentic kit, get on stage and do a turn.' The laughing suddenly stopped. 'Woody can teach us a few steps,' the DI added. 'What, you must be f*****g joking' came from more than one quarter, together with more than a few expletives. The DI gradually calmed the team down by explaining how well it would go down with the right music and strobe lighting and what the hell, it was only for a laugh.

But what could I do? What had all started off as a put-down for a flash little PC some months prior had returned to bite me on the arse. I knew absolutely nothing about morris dancing and even if I denied it nobody would believe me. And when the rest of team found out that the new boy on the block couldn't come up with the goods, they'd come to the conclusion that I'd put about the story to take the piss out of them . . . and I can tell you, there were some pretty rough characters on One Squad. Oh dear! Perhaps I could break a leg or go sick for three years. How was I going to deal with this problem? And who was the bastard at Plaistow nick who had told the DI the story in the first place?

Salvation works in mysterious ways because a couple of days later I met a pal of mine, DC Lenny Faul, and although we'd not actually worked together in the Met, he lived in the next village, so I'd known him for a couple of years. Now, I want you to remember his name because later on he makes a significant contribution to this story. Over a few pleasant drinks in a small country pub in Essex, one evening, Len wanted to know all about my new life on 'The Sweeney' but noticing that I was preoccupied, he asked the reason. Shamefacedly, I blurted out my tale of woe regarding the task that I was unable to fulfil at the Christmas Flying Squad do at Quaglino's, in the West End of London.

To my surprise Len drained his glass, put it down on the table and casually said, 'Don't worry, Woody, get another round in and I'll solve all your problems.' Suddenly, I became extra-cautious, as he wandered off into another bar, because I wasn't the only CID officer around to be the subject of an unusual story. The one I had heard about Len was that he and another Aid to CID, named Dick Kirby, had been detailed by the CID proper to assist in an observation where information had been received that a gang of robbers were going to attack a building society at closing time. As the witching hour drew near, a CID officer came along and wordlessly handed them a pickaxe handle each. Len stared at his piece of equipment and whispered, 'Dick, what do we do with these? Use them to bash the villains or plant them on them?' Dick, who was older and rather more experienced than Len, pointed to the pickaxe handle that Len was carrying and there, stamped in large black capitals, were the words 'THE

PROPERTY OF THE METROPOLITAN POLICE, LAMBETH STORES'. 'I think,' replied Dick, 'that the second of your proposals might be a little inappropriate.'

So, bearing in mind that Len's judgement on the odd occasion might be construed as slightly flawed, I did wonder what words of wisdom he was going to impart, but I needn't have worried. I knew he only had my best interests at heart, which just goes to show that you shouldn't listen to wild stories and jump to conclusions. By an incredible coincidence, the very pub we were drinking in was Len's local and the home of the local morris-dancing team. Within minutes I was shaking hands with the team's captain, a 6ft, 15-stone bruiser wearing ribbons and bells who had learned from Len that I was interested in joining his troupe. Instantly, he invited me to the next practice night. For the following few weeks, I spent one night a week with the dancers in the pub in Blackmore in Essex, training very hard, whilst waving my stick about for England. Plus drinking beer by the gallon. God knows how I made it home at times. Another night would be spent with the rest of One Squad in the back room of a nick, behind locked doors, instructing the lads in the cunning art of old English morris dancing to the accompaniment of a certain Detective Sergeant Freddy Cutts on an old piano. For obvious reasons, the location was changed weekly.

Some weeks later came the night of the stag do. Over two-hundred Flying Squad officers, immaculate in their dinner jackets and black ties, duly paraded at Quaglino's up in town. A magnificent meal followed with all the trimmings including as much booze as you could drink. During the ensuing eleven cabarets, the other squads contributed to a vastly entertaining evening, including songs and party tricks but nobody would ever dispute the outright winner that night. Yes, One Squad, our fantastic success was easily the best of the bunch. Imagine, if you can, the sight of twelve burly, broken-nosed, cauliflower-eared thugs, with shoulders like oxen – and me, in the middle, of course. All dressed in black and white checked trousers (borrowed from the chef), white shirts crossed with red and white ribbons, a full complement of bells (borrowed from the Blackmore Morris Eight) hanging from every joint, carrying pickaxe handles (borrowed from the police store), wrapped in tinsel, and sporting WPCs hats, we pranced onto the stage under flashing strobe lighting and danced to Terry Wogan's rendition of 'The Floral Dance'. The dancing itself, of course, was a total disaster and didn't resemble any kind of traditional English dancing whatsoever, but for light entertainment, it was absolutely spectacular. The roars of laughter brought the house down, and it went on and on, so much so even the catering staff came out from the kitchens and lined the back of the hall and joined in with the applause.

Eventually, we skipped off the stage and the crowd leapt to their feet, roaring their appreciation, cheering wildly and hurling bread rolls in every direction – an unqualified victory. Once again, I had managed to pull it off, by the skin of my teeth, and of course with the help of a little tinkle of some very small bells.

Two months later by orders of the Commander of the Flying Squad our triumph was repeated at the Squad's 'Mums and Dads' night out, where all our wives and friends were invited. Again, it was at a top London hotel but this time with honoured guests including Michael Parkinson, John Thaw and Dennis Waterman from the award-winning television series, *The Sweeney*. The tremendous ovation easily matched the one given to us at the stag night – and for about five seconds I was tempted into thinking that I might become the full-time choreographer for the Flying Squad, but there again, perhaps not.

I remember one of my guests that night saying to me shortly after my stint on stage, 'I'd love to dance with Parkinson, he's a real dream.' Still on a high, I just took her arm and escorted her to the top table, with a dozen or so bells hanging from my shirt, where a crowd of people were waiting to get Parky's autograph, and said to her, 'Just ask him' and she did. He looked up from his scribbling and said, 'Thank God, I'm sick to death of autographs.' He then took to the floor with a very grateful young lady who will never forget the night she danced with her idol at Quaglino's, all down to me of course!

However, the day job beckoned so the tinsel was removed from the pickaxe handles and they were slung into the boots of the squad cars. This was very necessary equipment for us because the pickaxe handles were used not only to protect us, but also to bash villains during a robbery, or if they reached the sanctuary of their getaway cars, to smash every window and drag them out. Necessary, as I say, but not officially sanctioned. I mean, everybody, including the governors on the Squad knew we had them and turned a blind eye. Put it this way, if there had been a Squad ambush and one of the villains had got past me, getting clean away, my furious Detective Inspector would have said, 'Why the heck didn't you clobber him with your pickaxe handle? What's the matter with you, not up to it?' It would have done no good at all to say, 'But it's not official, Sir.' I don't think he would have appreciated that.

Fate, who by now I thought was beginning to victimise me at times, had another treat in store.

Some weeks later serious allegations of misconduct involving another officer, who had allegedly taken a backhander, were levelled at the Squad and the Yard's Complaints Team was brought in to handle the investigation. It was nothing to do with me but in their usual ruthless efficiency the complaints team turned over everything that wasn't actually nailed down (and some things that were). So, one afternoon, into our office at Scotland Yard walked a team of detectives, sergeants and inspectors from the internal investigation department and detained all of us who were present. They also confiscated all the relevant paper work relating to their enquiry. I was marched out of New Scotland Yard with all the other officers and taken to an independent police station, where we were each interviewed separately.

I was interviewed over a period of four or five hours that night but, as I knew absolutely nothing about the allegation, I was eventually released, still with my warrant card in my pocket; an innocent man.

Some weeks later, however, I was hauled into the office of the detective chief superintendent heading the investigation at

Scotland Yard. As I took a seat in his office, on the tenth floor, he slammed down a pickaxe handle on his desk and demanded to know what this unofficial item of equipment was doing in the boot of my police squad car. Now, even police officers have 'rights' and these include the justification to decline to answer questions, so that's exactly what I did. The chief superintendent had obviously not heard of this propriety and went berserk, pounding the desk like an officer in the Third Reich, screaming that at the very least I had committed a disciplinary offence for which I could be returned to uniform. That threat alone was sufficient so I decided to capitulate immediately. 'Alright,' I replied, completely unnerved, 'it's part of the Flying Squad morris-dancing team's equipment, Sir.' That did it. The chief superintendent was, by this time, nearly foaming at the mouth and having great difficulty in forming some of the words, as he threatened me, time and time again. In a nutshell, he had completely lost it as a result of my last statement. By now I was terrified at the thought of being returned to 'the big hat brigade' so I sought to prove to this raving monster that taking the piss out of him was the one thing furthest from my mind. I pointed out the pinholes in the pickaxe handle, which had once secured the tinsel. It was at this point I saw, out of the corner of my eye, the chief superintendent's sergeant, who was there taking notes of the interview, discreetly turn away and cover his mouth as his shoulders started to vibrate up and down. The furious chief superintendent was by now completely out of control as he advanced towards me, round his desk, screaming at the top of his voice the most blasphemous filth I had ever heard. I stood up from my seat and discreetly backed out of the office into the corridor, which was by now full of typists, clerks and assorted police officers, wondering what on earth the row was all about. Naturally, I kept going towards the lifts and away, never to be seen again, at least not by that officer.

The years went by and the morris-dancing story faded from most memories, but not mine. After my retirement, at which I was given a cartoon of 'guess what', morris dancers, my wife and I went on a long-awaited holiday to Australia, returning via

Canada. There, in a pub in Toronto, we met up with our old pal Len Faul. Remember him? He had emigrated to Canada some fifteen years previously. Len had remarried and we and our wives spent the most marvellous and nostalgic evening running back through the events of the morris-dancing story for the benefit of Len's new wife, and the part Len had played at its conception. Everything was going fine, right up to the time that I returned to the bar, having spent a very necessary penny in the gents, quietly waiting to be served. There I was, standing there, not a care in the world, in a slight alcoholic haze, when I suddenly noticed an ominous quiet amongst the pub's clientele. Then the leader of the resident ceilidh band, who had been playing in the background most of that night, stood up and announced to the whole of the pub, which must have contained at least a couple of hundred people, that they had a guest from London, England. This distinguished visitor, he explained, was an expert English country morris dancer and would be delighted to demonstrate his skill, but only if there was sufficient applause! As the audience stood up and cheered I looked across at Len who sat there unconvincingly attempting to display both surprise at the announcement and concern for my embarrassment, and I realised I'd been well and truly set up, not for the first time, by Len. I accepted the inevitable. Luckily, I'd had a few pints by this point so I turned to the ceilidh band leader, on his small stage, and bowed. He nodded, and turning to the band, stamped his foot smartly three times and the band crashed into a boisterous (and quite inappropriate) Irish melody. As I skipped, pranced and waved my handkerchief at the audience, who roared their approval, I promised myself that this was definitely the swansong of the last of the Flying Squad Morris Dancers . . . or was it?

I often wonder what happened to that little snot of a PC who was the cause of this entire trauma, all those years ago. Perhaps he got his own just deserts by becoming a detective superintendent – on Complaints. If so, I'd like to think I had a hand in that appointment! By the way, as a footnote, the Metropolitan Police changed its regulations soon after: 'Pickaxe handles are now forbidden'. Regulation Mounted Police-type staves are now issued to the Flying Squad. It appears some superintendent in Complaints was responsible for the re-writing of police orders. This whole incident didn't seem to do my career any harm, in fact, within months I was promoted to detective sergeant.

Of course, I was still getting up to my old tricks, like the raid on a drugs factory in Hackney. At the briefing I was instructed to lead a team whose job it was to crash in through a side door of the premises, whilst other teams, at a coordinated signal, would simultaneously break in through the front and back doors. A simple, well-structured piece of police work. Well, yes it was, providing that the 14lb sledgehammer you were using was directed towards the correct door and not, as in my case, the one of the adjacent premises. Well, they were very close to each other and the same colour. Later that day when the local police turned up to inspect the wrecked door, which was by this time just hanging on by one hinge, I believe they blamed the damage on local hooligans – they weren't far wrong.

Then an informant of mine passed on some really 'top-quality information', at least that's what he told me. He said that a team of villains were stealing 'top-quality cars' and shipping them out of the country in containers, and by chance they were about to load a very expensive stolen car into a container the following day. As a result of this intelligence, I obtained a search warrant and organised part of One Squad to raid the scrap-metal yard in Canning Town, on the A13 in the East End of London, where the container was being hidden.

The following day, quite early, we arrived at the yard and produced the warrant and proceeded to search all the containers. Unfortunately, all three containers in the yard were full to the top with second-hand car and lorry engines, gearboxes and an assortment of spare parts, not quite the quality cars that we were expecting. This was going to be more complicated than I first thought, so a call for help was made to the Yard's stolen-car squad, experts in this field of criminality. They soon arrived and started to trace most of the parts as being stolen. All well and good, you may say, but they were used to being up to their armpits in oil and grease, which is more than can be said for the Flying Squad. Although we charged a few guys with theft, recovered a large amount of property worth thousands of pounds and broke up a gang of lorry thieves, I was gently reminded by the DI that the bill for cleaning all the suits of the team was not worth the aggravation, and not exactly in keeping with the Flying Squad's image. This bit of advice was politely imparted to my informant whilst I held him up against the wall, with his feet dangling in the air, at the back of a pub the next time I saw him.

The next bit of information was completely out of the blue. Shortly after the above job, the DI called all the lads up to the office at the Yard for a meeting concerning the annual visit to Royal Ascot Races on Ladies' Day.

It appears that on these occasions when thousands of people congregate in large groups, it is the best place to catch the highly organised gangs of pickpockets by the dozen, hence the reason for the Flying Squad to attend and hopefully scoop a few up. I hadn't really thought about it before, but of course it was obvious.

Then came the interesting thing. Each car on the team was given the task of acquiring pasting tables, wine glasses, sandwiches and even champagne. 'What kind of observation was this?' I thought, but who cares, it sounded terrific fun. A week later, on a glorious sunny day, all the lads met at Bow nick in the East End, all suited and booted. We then made our way down to Ascot race course in convoy in our gleaming, freshly cleaned squad cars which the drivers had worked on the previous day. On our arrival at the front gates of Ascot, the stewards, who were expecting us, just waved us all in, whilst other people in top hats and other finery had to form an orderly queue and wait to gain admission. Our cars were driven almost down to the racetrack rail. Talk about front seats. Within ten minutes the pasting tables were out of the boots of the cars and set up. Plates of sandwiches, wine glasses and of course the bottles of champagne were all laid out on crisp, clean, white tablecloths, compliments of the canteen at the Yard. Nothing for it but to enjoy the day and soak up the atmosphere. 'Pickpockets?' you may well ask, but whilst lying there on the grass bank on this glorious summer day, surrounded by hundreds of ladies dressed in their finest, this was the farthest thing from my mind. Unfortunately, fate again hit me squarely between the eyes.

Whilst enjoying the sights and sounds of Ladies' Day, glass in hand, a couple of us noticed an image of pure elegance in a bright-red outfit with matching hat, strolling in our direction. She had the dress sense and posture of a true lady, royalty even, and although she was some distance away, it was plain to see she looked stunning. As she draw level with us, she turned and obviously noticed her audience, who may have appeared similar to that of a group of 16-year-old boys ogling the new French mistress on her first day at school. This attention didn't seem to faze her in any way, she just smiled and continued on her way, turning heads as she passed by.

After a few more glasses of bubbly and a number of unsuccessful monetary visits to the bookies, it was time to make the inevitable trip to the loo, which I eventually located way back under the stands, miles from anywhere. I made it just in time. I dashed in and gained a prime position at the stalls where, with great relief, I proceeded to do what a man has to do, a man's thing. Then, whilst standing there, I became aware that I was completely on my own, so when I heard someone else walk in just behind me, I just casually looked round. To my horror, I saw the lady in red. Without so much as a by your leave, she walked straight up to the urinals, next to mine, and lifted her dress and produced an appendage, the like of which any man would be proud of, and proceeded to relieve himself, yes HIMSELF. It was about this time my attention was drawn to a rather damp feeling around my feet, and on looking down I could plainly see, not surprisingly, I had been pissing all over my shoes whilst I had been otherwise distracted. It was time to leave as quickly as possible whilst still trying to retain my macho Flying Squad image. Not easy, having just been the subject of another one of those seductive smiles from you know who. I grabbed my manhood and stuffed it back into my trousers not realising I hadn't quite finished what I originally went in there for, but there was no time to waste. I just made a quick dash towards the exit and my escape. It has never been known in the history of the Flying Squad for any member to ever back off any situation, no matter how dangerous, but there is always the exception to the rule. To this day bright-red dresses seem to put the hairs on the back of my neck on end, and if there is a hat to match, that's it, unabridged fear takes over, and I come out in a cold sweat, all of which I have kept very much to myself over the years, until now.

Chapter 5

Coming to Terms with Life

ife couldn't have been better. If work was wonderful, home life was even greater. With a lovely wife and three bonny boys, all doing well at school, life was just wonderful. I think this was about October/ November 1978, as if I could ever forget.

It was just this bloody heartburn that had been playing me up for a solid week that prompted me to go to my GP one evening. Purely as a precautionary measure because I was a smoker, I was sent to the local hospital in Harold Wood for a routine X-ray. Although I moaned, you see I was far too busy to do something so mundane, she insisted, in no uncertain terms. So, I went along that evening, but as it turned out, that visit was to change my life completely and so dramatically it makes me shudder at times.

Although the radiographer who did my X-ray that night wasn't qualified to tell me anything about what he had or hadn't found, he did insist I return to the hospital the following day to see a doctor. 'What was that all about?' I thought, probably found an old cracked rib or something.

Fate's a funny thing, isn't it? Just when things are going so well in life, there's a bloke in a white smock, a Dr Somebody, in a hospital smelling vaguely of antiseptic, saying things that you can't fully take in. Things like 'I'm sorry . . . it's lung cancer . . . You will have to come into hospital immediately.' I couldn't understand it. This kind of thing only happened to other people, not me. It's got to be a mistake. No, the truth was, I'd pulled the short straw this time.

Naturally, over the next week I had a number of tests, whilst I spent most of the day in the hospital bed 'shitting bricks'. In his office the following week, the doctor explained to Sue and me, 'It's gone too far, I'm afraid, there's nothing we can do . . . it looks like it may have affected both lungs. I suggest you go home and sort out your affairs.'

'Sort out my affairs? What on earth for, can't you give me a pill or something?' I replied. 'No,' he said, 'because, at the most, you've got about three months to live.' It obviously didn't sink in what exactly he was saying because I distinctly remember feeling sorry for the doctor, as he was obviously very upset. He tried to explain to me the gravity of my situation, bearing in mind he was only a couple of years older than me, but on the way home it hit me like a 10-ton truck, what he was trying to say.

How do you put down in words how you feel in a situation like that? The utter devastation, the fear so great you almost wet yourself every time you think of it, the shock to my family, my friends and colleagues. And of course my immediate family, Sue and the boys. So how do you come to terms with it?

How do you tell people, without falling apart in front of them?

Well, to start with you don't. You spend a lot of time crying, believe me, I did. How on earth is my family going to manage without me? There isn't a pain quite like it, the emptiness inside, the terror, it's overwhelming and it takes you over, every living minute. Total desperation, like drowning in the middle of the ocean and looking round and seeing nothing but emptiness.

Then, when your body can't take any more, you run out of tears. There's nowhere to go, nowhere to hide. You slowly try to pull yourself together for your family's sake and for your own self-respect, if you can find it, in amongst the dozens of emotions that are swimming about in your mind.

It's like climbing Mount Everest with a lorry strapped to your back. It's almost impossible to start and even harder to continue but over the next few days and weeks, with the help of God but mostly with the help of the best wife in the world, I started to gradually pull myself together and shape up for the next inevitable step of how to make adequate arrangements for my family, and of course, how to die with a little bit of dignity! Not because I was being particularly brave – I'm no braver than anybody else – but simply because I wanted to go out with a bit of self-respect. I wanted to walk the last mile in my life, not end up on my hands and knees and because there was no other option. There was no way, on God's earth, I was going to let my three young lads see their Dad crawl out of their life snivelling like a 2-year-old, knowing that would be their last memory of their Dad. So, I had to deal with it, somehow.

And it was no earthly use making all sorts of rash promises to God, because he'd already forsaken me. Hadn't he? How could he give me all the riches in the world, in the shape of my family, who I adored, with one hand and then take them away so cruelly with the other? I couldn't understand it, although everything at this time was so unreal. Death is never easy to deal with but when it's your own, it's even more difficult, yes you still feel the sadness but the fear of the unknown is overpowering.

Somebody up there must have been listening to my prayers because right out of the blue, whilst at home on my second weekend back from the hospital, I had an idea. An old friend of mine, a doctor who used to live across the road but had moved on to better things, might be able to help me deal with this. It was very difficult to talk things through with Sue and the family, as they were too close. Day to day things were alright, but it was the long-term aspects, like three months time, I found so hard. I just tended to break down, emotions just swelled up inside. I needed to get a grip. I needed professional help, someone who was detached but understood the pain, worry and mental torture I was going through.

The friend, Dr Peter Crawford, was by now head of the brain surgery department at Newcastle General Hospital. Rather apt. I rang him one Sunday night whilst at home and blurted out my predicament. I'll never forget it, standing there in my hallway speaking in hushed tones so as not to be overheard. I didn't want to upset Sue; she had enough to think about, her world was about to fall apart.

Well, after a short silence Peter said, 'Can I call you back, John, I am just in the middle of something?' I said, 'Goodbye' and replaced the receiver on the phone, another let-down. Not what I was expecting, but perhaps he also needed time to take it all in. 'Well, not the best idea I've ever had' also went through my mind but within twenty minutes he had called me back and told me to go to the London Teaching Hospital in Whitechapel the following morning with my overnight bag. They would be expecting me.

It appears he had spoken to one of his old medical school friends, now practising at the London Hospital and head of the heart, chest and lung, or thoracic, department there. He had arranged for me to be transferred from my local hospital at Harold Hill, where they had given up on me, to the London Hospital. All this in twenty minutes on a Sunday night. Now, that's what I call influence.

The following morning, as arranged, I made my way up to the London Hospital in Whitechapel. At the reception desk I was told to report to Royal Ward, where I was shown into a side room by Sister Royal, a real old-fashioned matriarch, who instructed me to undress into my pyjamas and get into bed and await a visit from the doctor. Within an hour I eventually met my new-found friend and consultant, Terry Lewis. There was something about the man; he had a presence that just commanded respect and trust. It made you feel safe for some reason, just what I needed at the time.

He arranged for me to have a very thorough examination over the next two days. This included running up and down stairs whilst testing my breathing rate, three or four X-rays from all different directions and what appeared to be pints of blood for numerous tests. Then at the end of Tuesday afternoon tea he called me down to his office on the first floor, where we both sat down. He placed his hand on my shoulder and said, 'I'm sorry, John, but it's bad news.' This was not completely unexpected, as I'd already been told what my prognosis was at the other hospital, three months to live if I was lucky. 'Yes,' he continued, 'there's no way round it. I've got to operate tomorrow and take out the whole of your left lung.' 'But, but' was the only thing I could say.

He continued, 'Well, with just one lung, life will have to slow down dramatically; no Flying Squad for you my lad, plus your chances are only 50:50 of making it through the operation as the cancer has taken quite a hold.' At this stage I would have jumped at a 100 to 1 chance, never mind an evens chance.

Now I know what a condemned man feels like, when just as he's being led out across the yard to the gallows, he spots the prison governor running across the courtyard waving a reprieve from the Home Secretary.

With a little bit of trepidation on my part, the operation went ahead the following day and was a total success. Dr Terry Lewis had performed a miracle as the cancer had almost spread from my left lung to my throat where they join up together, but luckily he just managed to separate the two lungs before that happened. He later told me it took him and his team about five or so hours to complete the operation. He said it was like decorating the hallway of a house through the letterbox. It appears he pulled apart some ribs to get into my chest cavity and remove the whole of the left lung. I remember coming round from the op and trying to ring Sue, who was at home with the three boys. With tears in my eyes and a lump in my throat, I shouted over the phone, 'I'm still here, I made it.' I looked a little lop-sided and was in a lot of pain, and for the life of me I had one hell of a job trying to remember things like my own bloody home phone number. It was the anaesthetic of course. I wasn't fully awake for some hours after, plus it was so hard to breath with only one lung, it felt like a steel band round my chest. I just couldn't take a deep breath, it was so painful. Over the next few days, however, the physiotherapist soon showed me how to breathe differently by using my diaphragm and not my upper chest like most people, which seemed to help. Now it comes quite naturally these days.

Another trick that helped the pain was to place a pillow under my left arm to support my sagging left shoulder, but walking around the hospital ward after a few days in bed was no joke. All day with a pillow tucked under your arm like a roll of carpet wasn't fun. However, it turned out to be a great experience as I gradually found new friends in the same ward in much the same circumstances as me, with the same fears and anxieties, and, in most cases, a tremendous amount of courage, which spread and lifted everybody, it was infectious. There was one old boy, who had gone though half a dozen cancer operations, who every time I passed his bed would say, 'Come to change my pillow son?' In fact, he was a source of tremendous inspiration. I recall him saying to me at one stage, when I was a bit low, 'Always remember the big red bus son.' What was that all about, I asked? He then explained, 'Whenever you think you're running out of hope and life seems too hard to bear, just remember the amount of effort the doctors and the staff put in, they haven't got the luxury of time on their side to worry about your slight depression and how you feel. They have a job to do and not a lot of time to do it in. So, when you think you're a touch low, just go out and find a big red bus and jump in front of it, but if you haven't got the bottle to do that, then pull yourself together and don't waste everybody's time in here.' That certainly gave me a kick up the pants when I needed it, and it worked, I never felt sorry for myself again, and if I ever do, to this day, I remember 'the big red bus'. Sadly, two months later he died, but I still recall his wise words.

Then came the next step, a short period of convalescing, about ten days. It wasn't too bad for me, lying in bed most of the day, passing the time with the other lads in the ward. A couple of them popped off during my stay but the remaining lads were quite a hardy bunch considering the circumstances. It must have been worse for Sue, life out there still had to go on. The boys still had to go to school every day. The cleaning and shopping still had to be done. I know she had a lot of support from family, friends and neighbours, who would offer to look after the boys in the evening so she could visit me in hospital, but she must have had times when she wondered what the future held for her. It was the times when you're all alone at night, with nothing but your thoughts to keep you company, that I felt for her and wondered how she was managing. How she was dealing with it, all alone, in our bed. How she was coming to terms with the prospect of possibly bringing up a family on her own. All sorts of things go through your mind in the long hours of the darkness and fear, just before dawn breaks to herald a new day. One more day, please God, one more day, then the clatter of bed pans would pull me round, as morning tea was served, and I discreetly wiped away a lonely tear and sat up in bed and acted like a proper man and faced the world.

Then, about ten days later, Terry Lewis, the consultant, came to see me in the ward. Again, he sat me down, as if for a general chat and said, 'John, you've done so well, but again bad news I'm afraid.' Well, I think my heart stopped this time. I didn't really want him to say another word; I am certain I felt a warm sensation running down the inside of my leg for the second time in my life. I didn't want to think about failure, I was feeling better by the day. He continued, 'We need your bed, mate, I've got some really sick patients coming in so you're going home, mate, to continue your recovery.' Well, I didn't know whether to kiss him or strangle him, even in those dark days humour was so important.

So, the following morning a Flying Squad car, driven by one of the lads, was waiting outside the London Hospital to take me home, courtesy of one of the governors on the Squad, at the Yard. I was home about a week and a half, during which time I must have had the world and his wife round to visit me. Friends, neighbours, fellow lodge members and, of course, lads from the job, plus most of my close family from all over the country. It obviously took it out of me because one morning, about ten days after leaving hospital, I woke up with this crushing pain in my chest. I could hardly breathe. Sue called the local doctor in, who immediately suggested hospital. With not even enough time to call an ambulance, Sue and the doctor bundled me into my car and Sue raced me back to the London Hospital in Whitechapel in East London, were I was expected following a phone call from the doctor. I was admitted straight away. They said I was bleeding internally so they had to put a drain into the side of my chest.

Now, here comes a very strange thing, which, to this day, I still find difficult to believe. As I was lying there in a side ward,

I can remember very clearly a doctor working frantically, almost panicking, down by my left side, obviously trying to get the drain in the side of my chest to work, but strangely I felt quite at ease with myself. I had this feeling of drifting away. In fact, I recall saying quite calmly to the doctor at the time, 'I'm going to leave you now.' A funny thing to come out with, but there you are. I suddenly felt so tired and I just drifted off. The next thing I remember was being aware of drifting upwards and leaving my own body and looking down on the doctor still working like mad on the body lying on the bed, which looked strangely familiar. Yes, unreal, but the feeling of peace was overwhelming and so warm and comforting. Then there was this white light, which was drawing me ever closer to its centre, nothing but peace. It is the only way I can describe it, certainly no panic or fear.

The next thing I remember is waking up the day after, feeling absolutely exhausted. I felt I'd just done ten rounds with Mike Tyson in the ring but that experience of drifting away took a few days to get over, I can tell you.

This time the doctors wouldn't let me go home for a while. So, I had to endue another two weeks in hospital. I sometimes wonder, even today, many years later, when lying in bed at night when I can't sleep, if it was all a dream but two things come to mind. First, why would I want to dream about that kind of 'out of body experience' rather than my family, and, secondly, why was it so real? I've come to the conclusion that when my time does come (at the age of 104 years) I don't think I'm going to be particularly scared to die and meet my maker, knowing what I know. But, of course, missing my family will undoubtedly cause me the worst pain.

That reminds me. During my hospitalisation, I received a number of visits from the Sweeney personnel, who, having obtained the permission of the matron, or so they said, would take me out for 'a breath of fresh air'. The fresh air lasted as far as the saloon bar of the Blind Beggar pub in the Whitechapel Road, East London, frequented by the Kray twins some years previously and the venue of the murder of their associate

George Cornell in 1966. But now, there I stood, surrounded by some of the toughest characters in the East End, pint in hand, clad in a garish suit of paisley jim-jams and slippers. Now, that's what I call image! It was so nice to get away from the hospital routine, even though it was only for an hour. The tricky bit came a few pints later when I was re-inserted back onto the ward. There to face an understandably furious matron.

With years of cunning and experience behind them, my colleagues from the Sweeney drifted away into the distance, leaving me in an alcoholic haze to receive the full weight of the matron's fury and, of course, the adulation of all the other patients in the ward. The swinging door, into the ward, was the only clue that my mates had even been there, apart from the slightly slurred speech of a rather unsteady patient smelling strongly of drink, standing in the middle of the ward, wondering if he had 'pissed tea', whoops!, or should I say missed tea, as he staggered back to the comfort of his bed and a bit of afternoon shut-eye.

So, with mates like that and the hundreds of friends who appeared from every conceivable direction and, of course, my loving wife and family, I crawled out of that black hole and back into the world of the living where, since then, I have greeted the dawn of each new day with considerable affection.

There then followed months and months and months of chemotherapy. This was another ball game; in fact, it was worse than the cancer and the operation put together.

An injection every three to four weeks, at the London Hospital, and then I'd dash back home in a Flying Squad car, courtesy of my team detective inspector. Within an hour or so the injection would take effect and made me sick, not just like an upset stomach, but almost turning myself inside out. The chemo was destroying, amongst other things, the lining of my lower stomach, which produced an acid-like bile that my body rejected, so I threw up, but it was burning my throat like hell. So, it was incredibly painful as well as being extremely exhausting, leaning over the loo, hanging onto the walls by, what seemed, my fingernails, turning my body inside out.

This sickness happened each hour on the hour for about two days and nights, during which time I lived in the spare room up stairs, curtains pulled, in the dark, out of the way, with strict instructions to Sue not to let the boys see me. I couldn't stand to see the look of horror on their little faces if they saw this skeleton of a man that used to be their fun-loving, outgoing, sport-obsessed father.

I don't remember much of what I thought about during those hours and hours of pain, in the dark, except I recall feeling very much on my own, just me and my thoughts. I wasn't, of course, Sue was always on hand. It just seemed that way. Loneliness is not a thing I've ever been able to deal with easily.

I suppose sheer exhaustion at times brought relief from the pain and those dark thoughts in the back of my mind that I dared not go to. I would force myself, whilst in this semi-conscious state, to think of happier days, back in Leytonstone as a PC in the late sixties, when there was no pressure or problems, just fun in and out of the job. It's funny the things that come to mind. For instance, it was about the time when all reported crimes were classified into two areas: major crimes, which were dealt with by CID, and minor crimes, which were dealt with by us uniform lads or wooden tops, as we were known then.

It was early January 1968 when I was given my first minor crime as a uniformed officer, the theft of a car. I wanted to do this right, so I took all the relevant statements and then religiously recorded all the details and submitted them to the Central Vehicle Index, or CV1, at New Scotland Yard. Any check being made anywhere in London or the Home Counties on that car, for any reason, would show the car as a stolen vehicle with me as the officer dealing with the investigation. I also carried out local enquiries to trace any possible witnesses but to no avail, a dead end! What a great start to my 'Super Cop' image, which I must admit was nowhere in place at this stage of my career.

A couple of days later there came a message from CV1 to the effect that my stolen car had been found abandoned, jacked up on bricks, minus all the wheels, in a car-park area overlooked by a small block of flats in Woodford, about 2 miles away from where it had been stolen. Could this be the breakthrough I was waiting for, I wondered? Later that afternoon I went to the car park and surveyed the scene. Looking up at the five floors of flats that overlooked the car park I wondered how many possible witnesses would just say, 'Sorry, I didn't see anything', 'No, I can't help.' But undeterred I decided to persevere and ring the door bell of the first flat and, yes, I was right the first time, as expected, 'Sorry', again 'Sorry' and so on. After two hours and five floors I was ready to give in to apathy and call it a day, but this was the last door, so what the hell.

I rang the doorbell. The door opened and standing there was a little old lady, every one's idea of 'granny', grey hair, pinafore and a charming cockney accent, not unlike my own. 'Come in, laddie,' as she walked back into her flat leaving the front door open. 'Wipe your feet,' came from the kitchen just as I got half way down the hall and so I dashed back to the mat at the front door.

'Two sugars is it?' she said, as she nodded in the direction of a hot steaming cup of tea. 'Yes please,' I replied gratefully. 'Just like my grandson,' she said. I then asked, 'I wonder if you could help me?'

She interrupted, 'You know he's in the Army?' 'Who?' I asked. 'My grandson,' she replied. 'Oh, very nice. I wonder did you see that light-coloured car down in the car park?' I asked. 'He's got one you know?' she said. 'What?' I replied. 'My grandson, that's him in the photo by the fireplace.' She pointed at a silver-framed photo with great pride. 'Very nice,' I replied and continued, 'Did you . . .'. I was stopped in mid-sentence by a large cup of tea and a fairy cake being lowered onto my lap, which I carefully balanced on one knee whilst sitting on a settee.

I continued, 'The car in the car park, did you see it arrive?' 'No,' she said. 'And the driver?' 'No,' she said. Great, I thought, my last witness and she didn't see anything. 'But I did see the other car, just like my grandson's blue Cortina.' At this point the conversation became even more confusing. 'What other car?' I said. 'The other Cortina which took the wheels from the first car,' she explained.

'Did you see that one arrive?' 'No,' she said.

Another dead end. Time to leave, I thought as I looked down at the cup of tea still balancing on my knee. 'But I did see him leave after he took the wheels,' she continued, 'he looked just like my grandson.' This was too much for the teacup to take; over it went, in the middle of my lap and I was left feeling more than a warm glow in my nether regions, I jumped to my feet with a sharp intake of breath.

I continued, 'But you were five floors up how could you see him?' 'No, silly, I went shopping later and saw him leave in the Cortina. Blue, yes, light blue, just like my grandson's,' she explained.

At this point I was standing there with a very dark, steaming patch in my frontal area, and still in a little pain, but I carried on, 'The index?' I said. 'What's that?' she asked. 'The number on the front of the car,' I explained. 'Oh, yes,' she said as she pulled out her pension book from a sideboard drawer. There, would you believe it, written right across the front page was an index number (from memory I think it was something like 'A377 ★★★').

'There it is.' I gently took the book from her, as evidence, and leaned forward and gratefully kissed her on the cheek. 'Oh! Young man!' she said. As I left the old lady's flat I felt success was mine. I had the index of the second car, and a description of the driver who stole the wheels from the first stolen car, which was my stolen one.

I dashed back to the station to trace the driver so I could go round and arrest my first big villain, all down to my own hard work. What could go wrong I thought?

But CV1 soon told me that the index had also been reported stolen five weeks before my one. So, what did I have: two stolen cars, one still outstanding, and one suspect, who probably stole both cars?

The chances of seeing the outstanding stolen car, a light-blue Cortina, one of the most common makes of cars at that time, driving around London, let alone Leytonstone, whilst I was walking my beat was about as good as winning the lottery today

– forget it, I thought, but I couldn't. The index was imprinted in my mind, probably because it was my first criminal investigation, and it was my only link to the driver of my stolen car, albeit I had recovered it, minus the wheels of course, and the thief was still at large.

Remember, I mentioned earlier I have a tendency to trip over luck rather than find it in blaze of glory? Well, some two weeks later I was on my beat, about lunch time, just casually walking up the road enjoying the little bit of sun that day, when I noticed an old man with a stick trying to cross the main road near a busy junction in the High Road, but all the traffic was far too busy to stop to let him cross. 'Super Cop' to the ready! I stepped out into the middle of the road, raised both hands and halted the traffic in all directions, within seconds I had caused complete and utter gridlock, but this allowed the old man to cross the road, to a small ovation from some bystanders who had noticed the mayhem caused by this plonker in uniform.

As I stood there in the middle of the road with both hands in the air, I noticed just two cars back in the line of traffic I had brought to a halt was a light-blue Cortina. Of course, I looked at the index, and although it was partly hidden, I could just make out 'A377'. I cautiously walked down the line of cars towards the Cortina. The driver's door opened slowly as I reached the bonnet and quickly looked down to check the index once again. It was the stolen car! I couldn't believe it. I dashed up the side of the car to find the driver's door fully open and caught a glimpse of a figure dashing off between the lines of cars.

In a flash I took up the chase, diving across car bonnets in true Hollywood style, a magnificent sight for all the onlookers, who had by this time grown to a dozen or so.

In the films, the hero, say Clint Eastwood as 'Dirty Harry', would have chased and captured the villain but in real life, nothing of the sort. This guy had a head start and was wearing trainers, jeans and a jumper, whereas I was in regulation boots, full uniform, top overcoat and of course a police helmet. But I did have one advantage up my sleeve: the cry that has rung out over many years across the silver screen courtesy of many a hero, 'Stop thief, stop that man.' Now I look back and cringe with embarrassment but the villain was making good his escape. He was much faster than me. Was this how it would end?

Fortunately, I simply tripped over even more luck in the form of a very large shape walking up the road towards us. He appeared to be the size of a truck, slowly walking towards my fleeing car thief. As the two of us got closer, this hulk of a man got larger and larger to the point where he appeared to take up the whole of the pavement. Although this man may have been slow in movement, mentally he was sound as a bell because my shouts for help to stop the thief had been heard, either by him or by my guardian angel that had prompted him. Whatever, the hulk raised his arm and promptly bashed the fleeing suspect with a blow across the head, which would have been capable of flooring four or five men.

As the young man I was chasing crumpled to the ground groaning, I, 'Super Cop', reached the spot and jumped on him absolutely exhausted, totally out of breath, I was finished. I then looked up to see the hulk saluting me in a smart military fashion as he walked away and disappeared into the crowd. It seemed like a lifetime before I got my breath back, enough to put my newly acquired prisoner in an arm lock to await the arrival of the cavalry.

Within minutes I was surrounded by flashing blue lights and dozens of coppers who soon escorted the prisoner and myself, plus the stolen Cortina, to Leytonstone Police Station to shouts of 'Well done, Woody' and 'Great job, we heard you screaming down your radio for help' coming from some of the officers. Of course, I just smiled as if it was all in an ordinary day's work. What I didn't know, as a very young and naive copper, was that excitement had taken over. I had to come down to earth and think about the next step to take. This was the first prisoner I had actually arrested on my own as a result of investigating a crime allocated to me. I felt rather like a man in the middle of a minefield taking one step at a time with his hands over his ears and thinking 'so far so good'.

In those far off days most police stations had the old detective sergeant who had seen it all and done it all and our station was no exception. We had Detective Sergeant Arthur Baigent. I have many fond memories of the old chap, one in particular was an entry he once made in the crime book to the effect that access to a factory had been effected by means of breaking a hole in the 'corrugated' roof, but unfortunately he had spelt 'corrugated' wrongly, not once but twice, so he crossed it out and then wrote 'crinkly tin roof'. Sadly, this ill-judged error was soon sized upon by a number of younger and less-experienced officers, who took the opportunity to humiliate him over many months. Why I don't know, he was just a nice old guy coming to the end of his career. Anyhow, Arthur sat me down as I explained the whole story to him from start to finish. Well, only the good bits of course.

We then both searched the Ford Cortina car I had recovered and found old AA books with names and addresses, index numbers and odd notes inside the covers, which was quite normal back then. Also the serial numbers of the radio in the car, plus bits of notepaper stuffed down the sides of back seats, which can reveal a wealth of information. Letters, bills, notes, telephone numbers and so on.

I then witnessed a great lesson in police work, an interrogation by an expert. Well, the sergeant was fairly average really but to me, back then, he seemed outstanding.

Some three hours later, we found out that my young car thief was wanted all over East London for car thefts going back twelve months, plus dozens of other jobs. I think it was at this point I realised that if you put in a little bit of work, you normally get back some results. Like life really.

A few months later at Snaresbrook Crown Court I was present when the thief was sentenced to three years. His name was James Hunt. It appeared he was one of East London's most sought after get-away drivers, who, in his spare time, went out on the streets of London stealing cars for spares rather than buying them – just for kicks. And I know you are wondering with a name like that, but no, I don't think he then progressed to driving racing cars.

With a few more arrests and commendations my name was beginning to be noticed but not always for the best reasons. One incident in particular was on my first night duty on St Patrick's Day, which I treated with a little bit of trepidation as this was about the time of the introduction of the dreaded breathalyser,

As I set out on the beat that night, I was reminded by the duty Inspector, 'There are plenty of drunk drivers about tonight so be aware.' Now, having spent a few months in my new career I was quite confident on the streets of east London. In fact, to walk down the street in a newly pressed bobby's uniform, helmet and highly polished boots had begun to make me feel a bit of self-confidence rushing through my veins. As even back then the uniform police had quite a bit of respect compared with the ordinary guy in the street in the East End of London. It was more the name of certain detectives many of the villains were wary of, no doubt for very good reasons, as history now confirms.

As I strolled up Leytonstone High Street at about 10pm that night I was prepared for anything, well, within reason. There was a nice friendly atmosphere, a feeling of good will to all men. On reaching the Red Lion pub, opposite Church Street, which in those days had an Irish club upstairs on the first floor, I was not surprised to see a car drive up and park outside. Then I saw the driver, a small man in his thirties and his passenger, who must have weighed about 16 to 18 stone and was about the same age as the driver. They appeared to be clinging on to each other as they disappeared inside the entrance, which led to the Irish club upstairs.

Although I thought they were well over the limit, they had evaded the full weight of the law by just making it inside the club before I could reach them. Anyway, I thought as it was St Patrick's night and they were out of harm's way, let's use a bit of good judgement and call it a day, so on my way I went.

However, when I was returning to the station for my midnight break and retracing my steps by the Red Lion pub I saw the same two party goers leave the Irish club and go over to their car, still clinging to each other as if for support. I thought this was well out of order, as I'm sure they had seen me. I felt they were not only 'taking the Mickey' out of me, but, more importantly, out of the uniform. This, I just couldn't let go. I decided that if they got into the car and attempted to drive, I would stop them and breathalyse the driver. To my amazement they did just that. So I stepped into the road and raised my hand. Looking back, quite a daft thing to do really. Luckily, the car slowed down and stopped just feet away from where I was standing. I approached the driver's door and said, 'I have reason to believe you have been drinking.' I opened the driver's door, but as the driver got out, the passenger also emerged from the rear of the car and before I realised what was happening he had belted me so hard with a swinging right hand that I landed on my arse on the other side of the road. As I struggled to my feet this same big guy jumped on me and continued to punch my head and body. My radio, which was still attached to me via a hand-set wire, was flying about like a snake in attack mode. Eventually, I managed to retrieve the radio and call for assistance; well rather shout for help, 'I'm getting a bloody good hiding', as I tried to fend off the blows raining down on me.

It seemed a lifetime waiting for help to arrive as I struggled with this hulk of a man. Then in the distance I could hear the two-tone sirens of the police cars coming to my aid. On their arrival, it took four officers to subdue my attacker and put him in a van for transit to the police station, plus the driver, who was still staggering about the road whilst egging on his friend. I reached the police station some minutes later and walked into the charge room, whilst trying to stop the blood pouring out of numerous wounds around my face. The charge room is where all prisoners are processed and to find a riot going on was, to say the least, very unusual. It was also very unusual to see some six officers trying to control my big man on the floor, and they were not winning. Arms and legs were everywhere. Then I noticed the back of a head hanging out of the side of the mountain of bodies. Here was my chance to get my own back on the big guy. I drew my truncheon out, raised it above my head and aimed it at this head. Just as I was about to bring down the truncheon the head turned round and I saw looking up at me was my duty officer, Inspector Ken Meek. Have you ever seen fear in a man's eyes? I have! Looking back I feel sorry for Ken, he was a really nice guy, it was always he who got me out of all the scrapes I managed to find myself in.

However, some minutes later when order had been restored and the prisoners were in the cells the duty inspector, who was still shaking from his near miss, called me to one side and said, 'What did you arrest these two for?' I replied smugly, 'The big one for assault on me and the driver for drink-driving. I saw him stumbling along the road, and then he attempted to drive.' The inspector rolled his eyes up into his head and said, 'Didn't you notice the driver had a club foot and had difficulty in walking?' Oh dear! Another fine mess I got myself into.

Because my uniform career was quite often punctuated by similar incidents, week after week, Inspector Meek was instrumental in getting me out of uniform and into the CID as soon as possible, and looking back who could blame him?

In fact, shortly after, whilst discussing my future career over a cup of tea in the canteen, he suggested I should apply to join the CID. He told me that he would not only endorse my application to join the CID but he would also help me fill out my application form. I thought at the time what a nice guy being so helpful. He could obviously see the many advantages of moving me on to another department and the responsibility on to someone else.

Think of it, plain clothes, but still an impulsive know-it-all and gobby but now with image! God help the force and the general public, a Police Commissioner's nightmare. Talking of which, Paul Condon, destined to become the aforesaid, was a PC at the next police station to me, at about the same time but his life as a PC was reputedly not as rich as mine. In fact, from all accounts it was quite dull and uneventful, in comparison, shame! I had much more fun.

Which reminds me of a couple of events whilst still in uniform that happened on night duty. At times this can be a bit boring, especially between 1am and 2am. Too late for daytime crime, like theft or assaults, because there aren't any people about, but too early for burglaries, which normally occur between about 4am and 5am. So, this is the time when the bobby on the beat has to make his own amusement. In the early seventies police in London used a motorcycle called a Velocette, which had a water-cooled engine that was very quiet in comparison to the more conventional type of motorbike, hence the reason for its popularity amongst the police. Although we didn't have one at Leytonstone nick, there was one at Leyton Police Station, which would cover both police areas on night duty. On one particular night, at about 1am, I was having a smoke with another officer whilst parked up in a panda car by the side of the road just by a set of traffic lights, at the top end of Leytonstone High Road, when PC George Bennett pulled up at the lights. Now George was a bit of a wag at the best of times but unfortunately he had just successfully passed a driving course on one of these Velocette motorbikes and this was his first night duty with his new toy. It gave him the chance to experiment and to enhance his newly acquired skills of riding a motorbike. I remember he was so excited as he pulled up alongside of us. Bear in mind that it was about 2am in the morning and all the roads were deserted. No one was about, apart from cats and coppers. George insisted we watch as he showed us his new trick but as he accelerated away, a sports car came from behind us like bat out hell, well exceeding the speed limit. But as he overtook us the driver must have realised he had just passed a police car at great speed so he slammed on his brakes and stopped just in front of us as the lights changed to green. Of course, just in front of him was, yes you've guessed it, PC George Bennett on his motorbike, who was unaware of what was behind him. I looked at my mate in our panda car and thought this could be interesting. Not willing to disappoint his audience behind him, George, who by now was going at a fair speed, started to climb up onto the seat of his motorbike on one leg, sticking the other one up in the air whilst steering the bike with only one hand, shouting at the top of his voice, 'How's that?'

What a sight to behold, the acrobatic police motorcyclist performing death-defying tricks in front of a member of the public whilst riding down the centre of the road at that time of the morning. The sight was just too much for the sports car driver who veered into the side of the road and mounted the kerb before coming to a halt in someone's front garden.

Not knowing if the driver or his passengers were hurt in anyway, we pulled over to check, but as I leaned over the now stationary car and opened the door, I was greeted with a very strong smell of booze. The driver then exclaimed with a slight slur, 'Did you see that?' I replied, in a very slow and measured manner, 'What, Sir?' He then took a very deep breath and said, 'The copper standing on the seat of his motorbike.' 'Has Sir been drinking?' I enquired. Then he just sputtered, 'Yes, no, but oh Christ.' There's only one reply to that kind of answer, 'Oh dear, Sir, can you blow into this, Sir?' Still, we got another drink-driver, who was obviously seeing things, off the streets and out of harm's way. I recall he pleaded guilty at court a few days later and, funnily enough, he never mentioned the acrobatic police officer. He just said, 'I've given up drinking; it's affecting my mind.' No more!

On another occasion, some days later, also on night duty, I think at about 4am in the morning, a fellow officer and I were sheltering from the rain in a recessed shop doorway by a set of traffic lights. We saw a Post Office worker, in his uniform, pull up at the lights on his bike, obviously on his way to work. I suddenly had an idea and as we were just out of sight, I took off my helmet and put it under my arm. Then I pulled my big duty overcoat up over my head and did the top button up, giving the appearance of a man with no head. I then walked smartly over the crossing, still with my helmet tucked under my arm, right in front of this chap on the bike and at the same time reciting very loudly, 'Once more unto the breach, dear friends'. The sight of the headless policeman had the desired effect. The early morning worker took off down Leytonstone High Road at high speed, squalling at the top of his voice, never to be seen again. Unkind I know and I bet to this day he never used that route to work again. Ah! Great days. Coppers were much more human then. There wasn't so many 'jobsworths' about. You could do a good job and still be yourself.

One of the best things about being a copper in the late sixties and seventies was not only the security of the job but also rent allowance. I can't remember the precise amount but it was pretty good. So much so, I soon realised that the small flat in South Woodford was not substantial enough in order to qualify for the maximum amount of the allowance. As a result, Sue and I soon got to work looking though all the local newspapers searching for, well, something a bit more substantial in keeping with my new career in the force.

We soon found the answer. A chemist had a large, split-level, modern, three-bedroom flat to rent over the top of his shop in the middle of Chigwell Village, 200yd from the police sports club. An appointment was quickly arranged at the flat but to our surprise we weren't the only ones interested. Some forty other couples had also applied. No chance, I thought. At the interview the chemist said he had been so inundated with applicants that he had had enough of the hassle. However, as soon as he learnt I was a police officer and was prepared to keep an occasional eye on the shop premises below the flat, the accommodation was ours. Great, and, in addition, right opposite there was the smallest, quaintest pub in Essex, the Prince William, although it is no longer there. Just three minutes away was Chigwell Underground station. The flat was in a perfect location and, more to the point, was a much larger place to live, in a great area and all at no extra cost as the rent allowance covered it.

There was a small village feel about the place and the flat felt really comfortable. It didn't take long to fill the spare bedroom with a large 9lb baby boy called Steven, who, to this day, still sports a generous shape to say the least. In fact, next month Sue and I are flying out to New York, where he now works, to share in his fortieth birthday celebrations with his wife Louise. When Steven was born, Sue and I asked another PC at Leytonstone, by the name of Graham Banning, to be Steven's godfather and so began a long and happy, albeit sometimes interrupted, family friendship which continues to this day. In fact, unbeknown to either of us, we were eventually to become fellow 'brothers-in-LAW'.

To shed a little light on this I'll explain. After a long day walking the beat in Leytonstone, I often popped into the King William pub for a quick pint on the way home and soon met and was admitted into a small and select drinking school. None of the other members were coppers but all turned out to be Freemasons, a fraternity I knew absolutely nothing about but, nevertheless, found very interesting.

There were quite a few characters in this small group of friends. One was Harry, a man in his late forties with an eye for the ladies. On one occasion I captured him in Buckhurst Hill whilst he was coming out of a pub one lunchtime in the company of a rather good-looking, well-proportioned, mature lady, who was not his wife. He was obviously wining and dining her and didn't expect to be seen by me, especially when, at the time, I was posted to an unmarked police car on crime patrol in the area. I know I shouldn't, but I couldn't stop myself. I asked the two lads with me in the car to dash out and arrest Harry, put his hands up on the bonnet of the car, frisk him down, put handcuffs on him then put him into the back seat of the car next to me. Well, all went well. He didn't stand a chance. The two boys acted out their part beautifully, which caused quite a sensation on the pavement outside the pub as this was quite a well-to-do area. Incidentally, the lady who was with Harry had discreetly disappeared into the crowd and was now out of sight, possibly with, what I thought, was a guilty conscience. Anyhow, as soon as Harry had time to look round in the back of the unmarked police car and saw me, a look of relief came over his face, which soon changed to outrage as he realised what I had done to him and the lady who was with him. As I said, she had by then disappeared into the crowd, many of whom by this time were peering into the car windows at Harry who was still handcuffed.

After a few expletives directed at me, I let Harry go, who's parting word were, 'I'll see you later' with a few F's and B's thrown in, of course, all a good laugh. I was in the King William pub shortly after 6pm to impart the story to the rest of the lads, who thought it was a marvellous tale and wished they'd been there to see Harry's face, until the door burst open and in walked Harry, who by his expression was not amused. At this point I don't know, even to this day, if Harry played a blinder of a double bluff or if it was the truth, but he claimed the lady in question was not his bit on the side but was, in fact, his bank manager whom he had taken out to lunch in order to obtain a loan. At this point everyone in the company went quiet and looked straight at me. What could I say? I just had to put my hands up and apologise profusely. I never found out the truth. Was she or was she not, that is the question? The incident was never ever mentioned again in the company, which on reflection is very strange, as he never had a verbal dig at me for losing the bank loan. Perhaps he really did have the last laugh.

Another one of the lads in the King William was George, a lovely man, who seemed to live a double life, the family and work during the week, then on a Friday night he craved the excitement of the unknown. He often invited me out to clubs and casinos but I couldn't keep up with him on my meagre police pay.

One Friday night he asked me to get him into a members-only club near Loughton, Essex which had a bit of a reputation for entertaining well-known faces in the criminal world. I thought it wasn't a good idea at the time but he kept on and on, so I gave in and took him to the club, knowing full well they would let me in if I flashed my police warrant card. As expected, when we arrived and I showed my card at the door, we were both waved into the club. Now, although I was off duty, it was a good opportunity to take advantage of the situation and to have a good look around at who was there and see who was with who. A good bit of experience for a young detective but as soon as we reached the bar, one of the bouncers tapped me on the shoulder and said, 'The governor wants to see you up stairs.' All we wanted was a drink and a look round but we were captured, so we just followed the bouncer up the stairs to the main office where a rather large man was sitting behind a very impressive leather-top desk lit up by a single light above it, rather like a 1960s James Cagney 'B movie'.

'Ah,' he said, 'fanks for coming up. I've got a small problem perhaps you can help me out wiv it. I'm not sure what to do about it.' 'If I can,' I replied. 'Well, I've had a phone call, anonymously of course, that there's not a bomb in the club. What do you fink I should do?' I thought for a second and replied, 'Did you say "not" a bomb in the club?' 'That's right,' he said. 'Who have you upset lately?' I replied. 'I know what you mean, but that's normal ain't it?'

I responded, 'Well, the first thing is to think about evacuating everybody from the club as soon as possible. Then call all the emergency services out to try to search for any possible bomb, just in case.' 'Ah, that's my problem, we would lose so much dough over the bar by clearing the place without knowing, for sure, if there is a bomb in the club or not, and I don't want to panic the punters.' I replied, 'Well, that's my advice. It's your club.' and turned to go but as I left, I halfheartedly said to him, 'Bye the way have you had any aggravation in the club tonight?' 'Well, funny you should say that,' he said, 'we had to put a punter out the door earlier.' I replied, 'That's maybe or maybe not the reason for the call.' 'Come to fink about it the voice did sound familiar.'

George and I then left the office and made our way down stairs as George asked what were we going to do next, 'Get the hell out of here as soon as possible' and that's just what we did. Too much excitement for one night, I thought, and I needed an early night, away from any bombs. After a quick pint in a local pub just up the road, we wandered out into the street and as I looked up into the night sky, nicely relaxed and was about to say, 'What a lovely still and clear night', the whole place erupted, blue flashing lights everywhere, all heading for the direction of the club we had just left. At least the manager had taken my advice, although we hadn't heard a bang, he did the right thing, and so did we by getting out of the club before the arrival of the boys in blue. It may have been a touch embarrassing to be found in a club with that sort of reputation.

There was one other guy called Peter who would pop into the pub on the odd occasion. I didn't know him that well, but on the second or third time I met him in this particular company he mentioned in general conversation that he had a few large sporting umbrellas in the boot of his car that he had acquired and was selling them very cheaply. I noticed almost immediately that the atmosphere suddenly changed and there was a lot of coughing and sputtering going on. It was fairly obvious that Peter was unaware that I was a copper, so to ease the situation I just said I would have one, but I had to go to the loo, so I would pay him on my return. Off I went, giving the lads time to explain, in no uncertain terms, that he was trying to sell nicked gear to a copper. I returned two or three minutes later and, of course, Peter had gone leaving his half-drunk beer still on the bar. I did mention his absence but all I got was, 'Oh, he was called away a bit suddenly'. The next time I saw him in the bar was quite a few months later and, of course, the umbrellas were never ever mentioned again.

Within a few months, and with the help and encouragement of the lads from the King William pub, who had by now become firm friends, I was put forward and seconded at a meeting, up in town, and entered the curious and interesting world of Freemasonry and the worldwide family of Masons.

Today, as a holder of London Grand Rank I still enjoy my Masonic career, as does the PC friend previously mentioned, which came to light quite recently at a reunion. It's a funny thing when you come across an old friend who you haven't seen for some years and find out through general conversation that they have merely been travelling on a parallel road in life.

One other aspect of living in Chigwell in those days was the friendly neighbours. Amongst these were Len and Sue Binder, a much-loved older Jewish couple. I clearly recall Sue's hands and arms waving about, like a windmill, as she talked, forever, whilst her husband Len stayed in the background more, emitting the occasional 'Whatever, dear' when prodded by his better half. They ran the local hardware store, just up the road. We became very friendly, and in fact I taught their two sons to drive in my spare time, which reminds me of the greatest coincidence I have ever come across, a million to one possibility.

During a well-earned day off I happened to pick up the phone at home to call someone and I realised I had inadvertently broken into a crossed line, not particularly unusual you may think but on this occasion I recognised the voice. It was Sue Binder, up the road, who was talking to her sister who, I think, lived in Woodford, 5 or 6 miles away. I couldn't believe it, a crossed line with both parties known to me, and what an opportunity to wind these two lovely ladies up. I had to think very quickly to dream up some kind of story to catch them both on the hop. After a minute or two I coughed slightly, then there came a short silence from Sue and her sister, 'Who's that on the line?' one of them demanded. 'Oh just me, the listener,' I replied. 'Just put the phone down and leave us alone.' I agreed and said, 'Bye Sue, have a nice day, Sis.' That's what Sue called her sister, 'Just a minute, how do you know our names?' said Sue. 'He's only winding you up, he's just guessing or he's heard me mention your name,' came the reply from Sis.

Then came the bombshell, 'Oh no, Sue,' I said, 'I know all about you both, the shop in Chigwell, the two boys,' mentioning their names in passing, 'your husband Len. The cars you both drive.' Of course, all this knowledge was easy to hand if you knew them, which I did, being a neighbour. I concluded by saying, 'I must go now, I've got other people to listen to, bye.'

Well, the proverbial certainly hit the fan, as it were, both women then started shouting down the phone demanding how I knew so much about them and ordered me not to put the phone down, as if they could stop me. They insisted l gave them more information, they were well and truly hooked. All I had to do was wind them in. I just told them that I had been watching them both for sometime and I had a large dossier on them. This made them even more agitated than before, almost to fever pitch. At this point I just couldn't hold it in any longer, I said 'Goodbye' and then hummed the old song 'The policeman's lot is not a happy one' and put the phone down.

I had forgotten all about this amusing incident on the phone, when three nights later, at about midnight, my wife and I where awoken from a deep sleep by very loud banging on the front door of the flat. 'What the hell is going on, a fire or something?' I thought. Sue and I jumped out of bed and opened the front door to find Len and Sue Binder standing there in their night clothes, dressing gowns and slippers, with Sue's hair in curlers, with her arms crossed, and Len following behind in an old, tatty dressing gown. I think he was still asleep.

'It's been driving me mad, hasn't it Len?' as she turned towards her husband, who just said, 'Yes, dear' like an obedient poodle. She continued, 'It was you all the time, you little monkey,' she said, with a slight smile on her face, hoping she had got it right, and had hopefully uncovered the phantom on the phone. My first instinct was to deny everything and watch Sue's face as she realised she may have got it all wrong and accused an innocent person, but I just couldn't hold it back any longer. What a sight to behold, all four of us standing there, in the hallway, in our night clothes, in roars of laughter on the door step. Of course, we invited them in for a late coffee and a natter until the early hours.

Apparently, the whole family had been in turmoil ever since my little prank, so much so, Len hadn't slept for days because of the constant badgering from his wife, trying to get to the bottom of the mystery man on the phone and that song, what was it called? Then the penny must have dropped as I was the only policeman they knew. The episode was the talk of the village for some weeks as Len and Sue eagerly passed on this amusing little story to every customer in the shop that would listen and even those that wouldn't. They were great gossips at the best of times but this was something else.

Chapter 6

Can't Get Away from the Treatment

ike a clap of thunder, reality burst back into my life, as I opened my eyes, yes, I was back home in the little, darkened bedroom hanging onto the sides of the bed as I felt my whole body stiffen up as if like a cramp attack. Yes, the chemo treatment was still working its way round my body. Oh God, no. It's coming again I thought. The pain and the agonising twisting of my stomach muscles told me it was time to grab the bucket and prepare to spew out that acid-like substance into the bucket yet again. If this chemo treatment is doing to the cancer what it's doing to me, the patient, then it must be bloody good stuff, but could I keep this up hour after hour for a couple of days until it again eased up? After about ten minutes, a calming word and reassuring hand on my brow from Sue, who had heard me being ill, brought a little bit of sanity back into my world in that little, dark room at home. Peace again returned with the feeling of relief, in the knowledge I had at least another hour or so before my demons returned.

It wasn't easy to say, but Sue also needed reassurance, as well as me, during these dark times of stress. So, I would occasionally put my arms around her and say, 'We're going to beat this. It just takes time. We'll be alright, you'll see, trust me.' At that she would leave me to rest but as she closed the door to my room I could hear her start to cry as she went downstairs to spend yet another night on her own with her thoughts, in front of the telly.

In order to keep me from going mad with the fear of what could happen in the future, I had to practise and train my mind to forget what I was going though and transport myself into another world and think of happier times.

So, back to the late autumn of 1969 when I took off my dark-blue uniform for the last time and spent the next few months in plain clothes as a temporary detective constable, or TDC. I was now learning the ways of the CID.

This was a very different ball game. The hours, for a start, were nothing like I was used to. An early day meant starting at 9am and working to at least 7.30pm, that was alternate days. The late days still started at 9am but finished at 10pm. That's ten hours one day and thirteen hours the next. This took a lot of getting used to, bearing in mind I now had a young family. I didn't realise until years later how I missed all the special moments, the days out, the kick-about in the park, reading bedtime stories. That was only the half of it. I didn't see much of Sue either and I don't think she was too impressed with my new career, in those early days.

However, worse was to come. My first job was absolutely terrifying. I was sent to Ilford Police Station to work under Detective Chief Superintendent Burt Wickstead, who was known as the 'Grey Fox'. He was a man not only well known in the underworld but also by the press. He was a large man and a bit of a bully but a good copper. In fact, I once heard a story that a good villain was taken to the interview room screaming knowing that he was going to be interviewed by Burt Wickstead which would have undoubtedly lead to him facing at least fifteen years' imprisonment as a result. I did learn one thing from him, though, well, two things really. First, that reputations travel quicker than mere hard work alone. Secondly, a short prayer, passed on to me by one of Burt's subordinates who had known him for many years, which sums him up quite well I think: 'Lord, help me to be careful of the toes I step on today, because they might be connected to the arse I have to kiss tomorrow.' It had taken years for Burt to get to where he was and he made sure everyone knew it. On the other hand, I had been a detective for about five minutes.

Within days I was told of the annual CID dinner dance, a black-tie affair and all the senior officers would be there. Of course, Sue and I had never attended such a prestigious function before. Then the bombshell, as the newest officer to join the department, it was down to me to make a short speech during the course of the evening. What a terrifying thought. Standing up in front of all those people, high-ranking officers, their guests and dignitaries from all walks of life. I was beside myself with nerves but, strangely enough, also a feeling of vulnerability, a condition I had not experienced before. I suppose I was beginning to realise how much I didn't know about the law, all the paper work and all the procedures surrounding court systems etc. This CID bit was a lot different from ordinary uniform work.

A month later, however, the night arrived. With Sue, the most glamorous woman there that night, on one arm and a short script, which had been prepared for me, under the other, I attended my first black-tie dinner dance. Also on my table that night were three other couples I had invited that were not in the job, just so Sue and I had some friendly faces on our table. The meal came and went, then the speeches began and all the high and mighty said their piece. Then my turn came. I stood up to rapturous applause from my fellow junior officers and began in a somewhat trembling voice, 'Ladies, Gentlemen and Honoured guests', at which point, Detective Chief Superintendent Burt Wickstead exclaimed in a very loud voice, 'Come on, laddie, speak up.' This remark was met with complete silence from the audience as it was obviously uncalled for, but I turned and, without thinking, made my first mistake and said, 'Sir, whilst on duty you are in charge but tonight it's my turn to speak.' You could have heard a pin drop as the silence continued. Not the best thing to say in front of all those people but I think they also thought, like me, his remark was extremely rude and unnecessary. So, when a ripple of applause started, I might add, by the very man who had stopped me in my tracks, and gradually gained momentum, leading to shouts of, 'Well done' and 'Go for it, Woody', I thought I had been forgiven by the old Grey Fox. Who said reputations were hard to come by? Never again would anybody on that police division ever say 'Who?' when my name was mentioned, but was it mere notoriety or reputation? I think there is a very thin line between the two.

Chapter 7

Is Survival Worth It?

F rom nowhere came this tremendous feeling of the whole of my body twisting in pain as I felt the acid burning its way up from my lower stomach once again. Yes, reality had returned and I was back in the small, darkened room at home, bending over in pain, reaching for the bucket, as this molten larva spewed from my mouth. Again and again I struggled to be sick. It was like trying to turn myself inside out. Then eventually I could feel the muscles relax, as I slumped back on to the bed in a cold sweat which was pouring from most of my body. This was the best time, as I knew I had at least a short respite before the whole cycle started all over again. The question crossed my mind, 'is survival worth it?' and I had my doubts at times. But as I pulled the curtains back to look into the back garden I saw my boys playing football, unaware of what could shatter their young lives, and, of course, it was worth it. I must survive no matter what, for them and Sue, nothing or nobody could or would take them from me. Time to return to the world in my mind where pain and reality didn't exist.

It would take me about two weeks or so to get back to some kind of normality after each chemo treatment. First, by sucking ice cubes for a day or two, then on to dry toast for a couple of days, which was very painful, as the inside of my mouth and throat was so sore. So it went on until I could manage a decent, full-blown meal of lightly scrambled eggs.

Then just as I could stand up unaided, looking more like a prisoner of war from a concentration camp in Poland in 1944, the three weeks were up and I was due for the next treatment. I found this more and more difficult to face, both mentally and physically. I think I went from 11½ stone down to about 6 stone but at least I was alive. Strangely, enough I didn't lose my hair. Not that it was any kind of a priority, although it did get a bit on the thin side.

One thing that did happen, however, that has stayed with me, even to this day, is the fear of injections. I think it's called 'Pavlov's Syndrome' (he was a Russian scientist who trained dogs to eat only when a light came on at the same time as a bell rang, conditioning the mind to react to a given signal). In my case, it was the injections. I just want to be sick every time I see someone given an injection, even when it's on TV it's a kind of throwback, in my mind, saying to itself, 'Here it comes again, the "Chemo" poison.' I must say, I don't think I could have made it, physically or mentally, if it hadn't been for the non-stop, hands-on, twenty-four hours a day care Sue gave me during this time. And she had three boys, all of school age, and a home to run, together with this sick, old man upstairs, who was obviously going through a hell of a lot of torture. When asked, 'Who's the Governor in your house?', I always reply, 'I am, of course, when she's out shopping.' Oh, is that so true. She was a tower of strength and inspiration in those long, dark days.

Although they had always been in touch with Sue and me on a fairly regular basis, by phone, it was a few months later when I had a visit at home from a couple of lads from the Flying Squad. I could just about handle the chemo treatment by then and although I must have looked a bit of a mess, it was great to see them. They kept me up to date with the latest news from the office, it was that feeling of not being forgotten. I recall towards the end of their visit, during the conversation, one of them pushed an envelope into my hand and said, 'Enjoy next week.' What was he on about? I turned to Sue who explained she had arranged a week's convalescence in Jersey with some old friends, who had moved over there a couple of years previously and bought a bed and breakfast/restaurant business near a harbour. I think my parents had paid for the trip, and incidentally they were also going to come over to our place to look after the boys for us, so we could relax. The collection in the envelope from the Squad came in very handy. I think it was about £400, which by today's standards doesn't seem to amount to much, but then, thirty years ago, it was a lot of money, believe me! To this day, I still get my leg pulled on occasions by guys at work reunions wanting their money back from the collection that they put into for my expected demise.

The friends of ours in Jersey made us very welcome and had arranged for us to be taken out by various friends of theirs every night to different venues because they had to work in their own restaurant earning a living. One of these friends, would you believe it, was the chief medical officer for the local police in Jersey. I must say it is at times like this that you appreciate the humanity in others, when it comes to the fore with true consideration for their fellow human beings. You realise it's great to give but extremely reassuring to receive, a lesson never forgotten.

In the weeks and months that followed I came to think of that small, dark room upstairs in my house more as my cell, where I had to serve my time for some imaginary crime, rather than a spare room, which we rarely used normally. At least it gave me time to reflect and retreat back to happier times in my mind, with all the ups and downs of ordinary life that seemed so important at the time.

I recall the first time I was posted to CID night duty with, I should add, an old DS called 'Peter the hat' who had been in the job for about two-hundred years. There was nothing he hadn't seen or done, a man I could learn a lot from. I started at 10pm at Leyton Police Station, the divisional HQ. As I climbed into the car with Peter, he told me to drive to a particular pub round the back of the nick. On our arrival I parked the car discreetly in an alleyway, thinking we were about to start a surveillance in a long, protracted and high-profile case, but that wasn't what was in store for me. No, I was ushered towards the rear of the pub and up the back stairs and into the living quarters, where the landlord appeared to be expecting us. A glass of Scotch was pushed into my hand and I was asked to take a seat. The landlord was there with a few of his chums, all very amicable but as the night went on and more and more glasses of Scotch was downed by all, the dreaded grey mist descended and before long time seemed to stand still until the dawn raised its ugly head and we had to return to the station to book off duty. I remember driving home that morning feeling decidedly unwell and thinking how could I keep this up for a week. Luckily, it was just a 'one off', thank God, and the rest of the week went very well. Plenty to do and plenty to learn, interrogating captured burglars who were protesting their innocence but Peter's long experience in the job was just too good for them. After thirty minutes or so, they just crumbled and admitted all, including dropping fellow conspirators in it up to their necks. It's a funny thing, separate villains in different cells and they never come up with the same story. Why don't they ever learn and get their story sorted prior to being arrested?

Some weeks later, having returned to day duty, I was given the job of escorting a prisoner from Torquay in Devon, where he had been arrested, back to Ilford Police Station, where he was wanted for a number of confidence-tricks offences in the area. It appeared he had been living down there in Devon for some time under an assumed name with his girlfriend and her teenage son, who had been caught, by the local constabulary, riding a quad bike under age. When the local police turned up and wanted identification, he was captured, or rather gave himself up, because he didn't want his girlfriend involved.

All the arrangements were made and so I travelled down to Torquay the following day by train. This was fairly uneventful and on my arrival I was met by two local officers who escorted me to the Police HQ. I introduced myself to their senior officer on duty who suggested to these two younger detectives that they entertain this officer from London and take me out on the town as it were, in order to pass the time until the first train back to London the following day.

These two officers were eager to get to know the detective from London to see if he bore a resemblance to the portrayal of police officers on TV and in the press in those days. I didn't disappoint them when they took me out on the town that evening, with lines like 'shut it' and 'you're nicked Tarquine', all in keeping with the London image of the time. I soon became a minor celebrity in the local hot spots of Torquay, albeit finding it increasingly more difficult to stand as the evening went on. Towards the end of the night, we finished up in a Chinese restaurant somewhere, and that's the last thing I remember.

The next morning I was awoken in a strange bed in a strange room in a small hotel by the knocking on the door by the same two officers I was with the night before. 'Great night,' one said, 'especially your "singing and fancy footwork"', none of which I could remember. Within a few minutes we were on our way, accompanied by one hell of a hangover. They drove me to Torquay's main police station where I collected my prisoner, Mr Justin Roland Howard-Torrington, a truly old-fashioned con man; charm, style and professionalism were his middle names. His mere presence stood out in a crowd and so well dressed in a suit it would take me a year's wages to buy. I duly handcuffed him and took possession of all his property including his personal cash against my signature together with a large number of credit cards in numerous names, something I would have to sort out back at Ilford Police Station.

Transport was then provided to the local railway station by courtesy of my new-found Constabulary friends and we were deposited on a train back to London, hangover and all. Nevertheless, Justin and I soon settled down and once we were moving I took off the handcuffs.

Justin turned out to be a wonderful storyteller, all part of the art of a true professional con man but, of course, they do love to boast of their past accomplishments. Before long, though, together with the motion of the train and the easy tone of Justin's voice I had drifted into the land of nod. What could go wrong? You may well ask.

Sometime later and who knows at what time, I was awoken by the train jolting forward whilst leaving a station. I looked around and found myself completely and utterly alone. No prisoner and probably no career, or worse, posted to Uniform Traffic Police. There then followed a short period of shouting expletives at the top of my voice and pulling of hair, which seemed to help a bit. I then thought, 'What am I going to say back at the station? I lost a prisoner because I fell asleep?' No, I don't think so. What could I do? I could say he attacked me, and jumped out of the train. No, what else could I think of? Perhaps he was helped to escape by half a dozen armed men. No, my mind was racing round in circles.

At about this point I saw a lone figure passing the carriage door, carrying a tray of drinks and sandwiches. Yes, my prisoner! I shouted, as I opened the door, 'Where the hell have you been?' 'Just a little light refreshment, John,' came the reply in true gentlemanly fashion. I didn't know whether to strangle him or kiss him. 'And how the hell did you pay for that lot? You've got no money.' He looked slightly sheepish at this, but said, 'Oh yes, your change.' I'd forgotten he was an accomplished pickpocket, amongst his other skills; he'd lifted my bloody wallet as I slept!

However, anger soon passed to laughter as we settled down again to still more stories but this time I remained wide awake. I didn't even blink my eyes for the next couple of hours, during which time it soon became apparent that amazingly our paths had crossed before.

It transpired that some months earlier I had been following a van in Ilford which had just collected thousands of pounds worth of furniture from a shop, for which the driver had paid cash. This obviously made the shop assistant very suspicious, hence the police involvement. My instruction from my sergeant at the time was to shadow the van discreetly to see where it went and report back to the station, but the driver, for some reason, realised he was being followed. So, when he stopped at traffic lights on the A13, just on the outskirts of London, he jumped out of the van and made a run for it, leaving me with a van full of brand-new furniture, no driver, no owner, and no way of tracing the identity of either, as the van was hired with false documents. There I was, stuck in the middle of the A13 main road with a police car, a hired van full of furniture, no prisoner and no appetite for what would be months of being chased up by the station sergeant to make space in the property store at the station and get rid of all this furniture which I couldn't restore to the owner or driver, as he had done a runner.

The next few weeks became a complete pain in the butt because I couldn't get rid of the furniture from the police store room as it had been legitimately purchased. It was just, 'Who was that bloody driver?'

Now, back to the train, where Justin was recalling one of his exploits. The story unfolded that he had had a near miss with the law in Ilford whilst on the run when he lost a van full of furniture! Sitting opposite me was the very man that had caused me so much aggravation. Mr Justin 'Bloody' Howard-Torrington, yes, a wanted man, hence the reason for dumping the van but he was such a likable gent. How could you bear a grudge? Especially when the stories he was coming up with were so entertaining and, of course, I was making mental notes of all the details so that at a later stage I could make further enquires and classify them as 'clear ups' in the crime book back at the station. All down to my interrogation skills, of course.

But one particular story he recalled left me completely flabbergasted. It was so audacious I must pass it on. Not to do so would be criminal and a waste of a cracking story. You must understand, though, this is just between us and not to become general knowledge. Well, you know what I mean.

First, a little bit of background, as Justin would say. It appeared that the previous summer my gentleman con man had treated himself to a few days rest and recuperation at a resort on the south coast, where he stayed at a small guest house just round the corner from the High Street. This was run by a middle-aged landlady, who, in the winter months, closed the guest house down and did a little 9 to 5 job locally just to keep her ticking over until the season started again in the spring. During his stay there, Justin had the temporary use of a front-door key and, not being a man to miss an opportunity, he had had a copy made. Why, you may ask? 'Because you never know, old boy,' as Justin would say.

Now the scene is set, the con starts with a return visit to the same town but this time in the winter, knowing full well that the landlady of the guest house is out all day. Mr Justin Howard-Torrington enters a small High Street jewellers, just round the corner from the guest house and, as usual, he is immaculately turned out. He then proceeds to impart a most sorrowful tale to the owner. It would have broken anybody's heart. His story was that, although he and his wife of some thirty years of marriage had come from quite a poor background, he had, through hard work, become a very successful and wealthy man and could now afford to buy his wife a very expensive eternity ring. But here comes the tearjerker; he then tells the jeweller that unfortunately his wife is now in the last stages of a terminal cancer, so he would have to sell the ring back to the jeweller within a few months. Now, no con works without a little bit of greed and a good helping of a sob story doesn't go amiss either. Of course, the jeweller was hooked and starts producing trays of rings worth thousands of pounds. Justin just 'ums' and 'ahs' and then eventually says he can't make up his mind without his wife but she is too ill to come to the shop so could the jeweller close his shop a little early and come round to his house, just round the corner at about 4.30 that afternoon?

It's not every day of the week a jeweller, in the winter months, can sell a ring worth that amount, especially knowing that he may buy it back in a few months time at a greatly reduced price. So, naturally the jeweller agrees. He must have thought, what could go wrong? Justin then makes arrangements to call for the jeweller at about 4.20pm later that day and take him round to his so-called home address, in reality a six-bedroom guest house, closed for the winter. Justin still has the spare front-door key, of course, so on their arrival at the house, he lets himself and the jeweller into the house. It all looks very normal, especially when Justin kicks off his shoes and puts the kettle on the gas for a cuppa. He then proceeds to go upstairs to see his make-believe dying wife. In the meantime, the greedy little jeweller, who is very keen to take full advantage of someone else's supposed misfortune, is still sitting in the kitchen holding his briefcase on his lap, containing thousands of pounds worth of rings set in half a dozen trays. Justin returns with a tear in his eye, stating that his wife is far too ill to come downstairs to see the rings, so can he take the briefcase containing the rings upstairs to her? What could the jeweller say, he couldn't lose the sale, and in any case the customer is in his own house in his stocking feet with the kettle on. So, the jeweller agrees. With that, Justin goes upstairs with the briefcase and the rings, straight out the back first-floor window, down a drainpipe, round the corner and into the High Street and, to crown it all, he walks into a shoe shop, buys another pair of shoes and then away, never to be seen again.

Now you may well be asking yourselves what happened to the jeweller. Well, police temporarily arrested him when he was found in the kitchen, sitting by a boiling kettle, by the owner when she returned from work, just shortly after 5 that night. His story of the dying wife situation and his briefcase of rings wasn't readily believed by the police at the time and who could blame them. It all sounds too ridiculous to be true but there you are, there's nothing stranger than real life.

Some months later at Snaresbrook Crown Court, in East London, Mr Justin Howard-Torrington received a total of five years' imprisonment; he'd obviously charmed the judge because he was a career villain and didn't deserve such a short sentence. But over the few months whilst involved in the presentation of his case for court I felt I'd learnt quite a lot from a true professional career criminal.

Of course, I always thought I was fairly streetwise but sometimes it takes a little situation to make you realise that perhaps one has a little more to learn, especially when it comes from an unexpected quarter. One particular case comes to mind in the form of a little, old lady who was obviously born and bred in the East End of London and was certainly streetwise.

As I recall, I had heard a whisper on the grapevine to the effect that there was going to be a street robbery of a tallyman, you know, the weekly door debt collectors. Well, to cut a long story down to size, I told my detective inspector my informant's story and he promptly arranged for a team of us temporary detectives from the station to collect a nondescript van from an adjacent police station so that we could lie in wait, hidden in the back of the van, parked in the street at the appointed time and day.

A couple of days later I duly collected the van, installed its precious cargo of young detectives and drove round to a back street of Ilford, where I parked up the van and climbed into the back to await for the robbery to unfold in front of our eyes. A perfect situation you may think, but after about an hour or so in the back of this van with half a dozen guys it got a bit smelly to say the least. Then, completely out of the blue, a little, old lady popped up, banged on the side of the van and shouted so loudly that she could have been heard back at the station, 'I've put a tray of teas by the back door, lads, don't let them get cold.' So much for working under cover. It was very embarrassing climbing out of the back of the van feeling that everybody from every window was watching me pick up the tray of teas and place them on a small wall nearby, then getting into the front seat of the van and driving back to the nick, utterly deflated and dreading my next visit to the canteen, no doubt to be the centre of humorous banter, once again.

I think at the end of the day she was a bit more streetwise than all of us put together. Come to think of it, little, old ladies have had quite a large input in my life in more ways than one.

On another occasion I was in the office at Ilford Police Station when I took a phone call from a local dentist, of all things, who proceeded to impart such a story that I immediately thought, 'I should have gone sick today and had the day off.' The dentist explained that a man was travelling around the local area booking appointments with dentists but on his arrival he would insist that he was given gas before he opened his mouth because he was so nervous. Not particularly outrageous, you may think, but on getting the guy's mouth open the dentists would find a mouth devoid of any teeth whatsoever. This guy just loved having the gas; it was a kind of an addiction or fetish. So, he was a bloody nuisance but not really committing a criminal offence as such. I politely informed the dentist that this was more a civil offence and to take out a court order at a county court to restrain his behaviour and put the phone down, thinking that was a close

Looks good, but very gobby, still thinks he's on a building site. This photograph was taken at Hendon Police Training College, late 1967.

A half-asleep DC Woodhouse photographed by an undercover team from C.11 on the corner of the Old Bailey, 1970s. Whilst appearing to practise a QC pose, I'm ready to give evidence.

Working hard in the photofit office – paper, paper and more paper, 1997.

The presentation of the morris-dancing cartoon at my retirement party, 1998.

Golly, what a long wall you have and fairly straight as well, 1963.

Yes, you can tell by the pose, there's plenty of attitude. Holiday photographs taken in the early sixties.

Once a year on New Year's Day, a group of friends and I turn out and perform for charity. We call ourselves the 'Doris Dancers' – look carefully and you can see my police truncheon just below my banjo, 2011.

Sydney Harbour bridge on our first trip to Oz, 1998.

Never far away from the 'heavy mob' – Sweeney Todd means Flying Squad in cockney rhyming slang.

Just another family get-together. Three generations at a barbecue at home, 2011.

Just being nosey, 2010.

A quick clean-up during the building of my small, five-bedroom bungalow, 1995/6.

The Boss and I, 2004.

one, what could you do in a case like that? He was just a nuisance.

There I was thinking I'd got away with it again, but unbeknown to me the older and far more experienced Detective Sergeant Henry Naulls had picked up the phone in the other office at the same time and was listening in to my conversation on the same line. Within about thirty seconds I heard a loud shouting coming from the other office, 'Woodhouse, get your arse in here now.' As I walked into the other office I was fairly comfortable in the knowledge that no one else was in the office at the time I had taken the call and I had not given my name to the dentist. So, as you can imagine, I was staggered when the old sergeant said, 'Go round and see that dentist and tell him you've had second thoughts and have decided to arrest this guy and charge him with theft of gas, nominal value, in order to get him in front of a court where social services can get him some kind of help.' Now, why didn't I think of that? After a short lecture on the law and a flea in my ear I proceeded to go round to the dentist. He was very pleased to see me as this man had caused so much time and trouble amongst the dental fraternity that his details had been wildly circulated throughout the east London area, and in fact he had already made an appointment at another dentist just up the road for a few days' time.

Needless to say, arrangements were made and some days later I, plus one of the other lads from the station, were fully dressed in white coats waiting in a dentist's surgery at the allotted time to see a middle-aged man walk into the surgery and take his seat in the dentist's chair. He then insisted on gas being given before he would open his mouth. At this point, having been provided with his description, I stepped in and arrested him and took him to the station where he was charged with the theft of gas and bailed to appear at court later. No problem, you may think!

The following day I attended a packed Barking Magistrates Court, where I saw my prisoner walk into the court main reception area with bandages all round his head. Here it comes, I thought, a complaint against the police for violence; obviously his way of getting his own back on me. How wrong I was. On being called into court to give his account of the incident in which I had arrested him, he proceeded to claim he had sprained his brain and could not remember the circumstances of the previous day. You can imagine the total uproar in the court. Luckily, the magistrate saw he needed help and put him in the hands of social services and then proceeded to compliment me, as the officer in the case, for using such a direct and novel method of dealing with such a difficult case. However, my newly acquired self-importance took a bit of a dive when the news got back to the sergeant at the station that my prisoner had caused havoc in the court by stating he had 'sprained his brain'. To be honest, the whole job was a total farce from start to finish. It had to be done, but why by me? And why were there so many officers in court that day, as if someone had warned them that Woody had done it again by producing a live comedy show at court!

Talking of jobs that had to be done, some are quite difficult, as with this next case, in late 1971. A young lady made a phone call to the CID office, in which she made an allegation about a flasher (a person who indecently exposes himself). It appeared she lived on the sixth floor of a block of flats, and had witnessed a young man in the rear garden of a house overlooked by her block of flats exposing himself to all the occupants of the flats. Together with two other TDCs (Temporary Detective Constables), I jumped in the duty car and rushed to the location, just a few miles away, where all three of us dashed into the block and up to the sixth floor and rang the bell of the flat concerned. A very nice and shapely young lady, in her late twenties, opened the door and invited us all in. She explained that every few minutes, a young man would appear from a house, which she pointed out from her window, and stand in the garden, almost naked, playing with himself. At this point, she screamed out, 'There he is!' and sure enough, in plain sight for every one to see, there was this young man masturbating in his back garden, just below the window of the flats.

I should explain that in those days we TDCs tended to work in pairs, and took it in turns to be credited with any arrests, just to keep the total even over the week. Anyhow, it was my turn to show the arrest. From the sixth-floor window I counted the gardens down from the corner house and, together with one of the other lads, went back down in the lift and round to the house in question. We climbed over the rear gardens into the correct one and peered in at the rear window, where I saw a pimply face youth of about 15 years, naked in his living room, still playing with himself. I tapped on the window and indicated to him to open the back door, and after fumbling about for a few seconds, he did just that. Naturally, I arrested him and took him down to the station, where I called his mother, who was at work at the time, and asked her to attend the police station as he was a juvenile. I suppose it took an hour or two to take a full statement from this young kid and eventually charge him with the offence and bail him out to attend court at a later stage. But where was the officer who was left at the flats to take a statement from the lady who witnessed the original offence? He was fairly new to the office and was only attached to the CID on a temporary basis because he hadn't been in the job that long, so I was rather concerned, something must be holding him up, but what? Nevertheless, it was about mealtime, so, as there was no urgency, I just went and had some food in the canteen. On retuning to the CID office after my late lunch, I saw the missing officer who I'm not about to identify, the reason why will soon become apparent, and in any case I heard he left the job shortly afterwards. He was sitting at his desk. 'Got your statement from that woman,' he muttered as he passed it over to me across the desk. 'Why the delay?' I asked. 'No reason,' he replied, with a slight smirk on his face.

Months later I found out that the woman concerned was very unhappy in her marriage and obviously needed a shoulder to cry on. Anyhow, one thing led to another, and before long this fellow officer was visiting the young lady on a very regular basis. Not at home, of course, as they had had a near miss with the husband retuning home early one day, but at a nursing home, where she was the night sister. According to a reliable source, she wore black stockings and little else under her neatly starched nurse's uniform whilst on night duty. I don't know who worked the hardest on that job, me collating all the evidence, formulating the charge and report, attending court to give evidence, then dealing with the aftermath with the probation officers and finally completing the results on the kid's file before submitting it all to the governor for approval, or the repeated visits by that young officer to the nursing home, after dark, to offer comfort and sympathy to this very unhappy young lady. Well, perhaps not so unhappy now, having got such a high level of caring police service, which she undoubtedly appreciated.

At about this time I had to attend a number of courses as a TDC at the Detective Training School at Hendon, North London. These courses lasted a couple of weeks, depending on which one you were attending, the elementary or the advanced. They were not residential as such, but one could stay overnight if there was a lot of travelling involved, as some TDCs had to make their way to Hendon from the other side of London.

On one of these courses I met up with the first black police officer in the Met, Norwell Roberts QPM. His nickname was 'Nozzer the Cozzer' ('Noz' for short).

Noz Roberts was a very outward-going guy, a larger than life character – a little bit like me, but twice as much! So, being very similar, I would have thought there might have been a clash of personalities, but on the contrary we hit it off almost immediately. Before long we became firm friends, which must have been very hard going for the rest of the class, who would not have expected a black and white 'Two Ronnies' double act to take over the class every minute of the day throughout the course. Although he was a young copper just like me, he was also ready to take on the world and enjoy every second. There was always a fair amount to take in on these courses, so in the evenings after class it was nice to wind down over one or two pints of beer.

At this point I did wonder if I should mention this officer by name but as there was only one black officer around at that time it would be silly not to.

Noz went on to become an extremely successful undercover police officer for many years, and as a result was the first black man in the Met to be awarded the Queen's Police Medal for Distinguished Service, no mean feat for any officer. But in the days of the early seventies he had not reached that level of expertise, although I must say he did appear to have a natural flair for undercover work. This came to the fore on one of our evening wind-downs. It must have been fairly late one Friday as the two of us had already had a few drinks in the British Transport Police Headquarters bar at Kings Cross. We decided to have just one more drink for the road before we went home, so we popped into a local drinking club.

I recall asking Noz to get the drinks in whilst I made a visit to the gents.

On my return, I noticed Noz, who was sitting at the far end of the bar, in deep conversation with a very tall, thin black guy. As I sat down on a stool next to Noz, the black guy walked away. As I took a swig of my beer I asked what the guy wanted. Noz replied, 'He wanted to know if I wanted any Ganja.' 'What?' I replied. 'Didn't you tell him we are coppers?' Noz just shrugged his shoulders and said, 'No, but I did order enough for the whole class.' I could see why Noz was destined to become a very good undercover cop, he just had no fear and could think on his feet. He also tended to dress, shall we say, a little on the loud side. He always wore very leary kipper ties and a silk handerchief in his jacket pocket. There was more than a touch of bling about him, which went very well with his one gold tooth. But arranging enough drugs for the whole class was going well over the top, even allowing for his outrageous sense of humour.

Normally, when an undercover operation is undertaken there are a number of golden rules to be observed. First, to arrange an arrest team to be on hand to grab the villains and monitor the safety of the undercover officers, and, secondly, to have some marked cash to hand to show the villains as a prerequisite before they produce any drugs.

None of the above was in hand and more to the point there was no time to arrange it. Obviously, the nonchalant attitude that Noz was displaying had been mistaken for that of a laid-back professional criminal who was used to buying drugs on a daily basis, but in reality we were a couple of young guys on a night out who had had more than enough to drink.

But what next, leave early and avoid any problems with an unauthorised drugs buy because we had no cash or backup of any kind and could well be on the wrong end of a good hiding by the pusher's minders? This was the most sensible thing to do, drink up and go. We both looked at each other, but I knew by the smile on Noz's face that wasn't what he had in mind.

I knew instinctively this was going to end in trouble but I managed to get Noz to drink up and leave the club. Outside in the car park we were discussing our next move when I spotted a lifeline in the form of a PC walking on the other side of the road. I thought this could be our way out of a very tricky situation. I persuaded Noz to follow the PC further up the road and out of sight of the club where we stopped him. After a couple of minutes explaining to the PC who we were and the situation we had found ourselves in and the impending arrival of a car in the car park of the club down the road, with its load of drugs on board and no doubt a tall black guy together with an assortment of minders.

We could see by the expression on the PC's face, he was completely out of his depth. So we suggested he contact his local police station via his radio with a request for immediate backup to stop and search the suspect car on its arrival. There was obviously someone at the station with a bit of know-how and a sense of urgency because within a couple of minutes a van fully loaded with seven or eight PCs arrived just up the road. It stopped and turned its lights off and waited for the signal to swing into action.

By this time Noz and I had sobered up slightly and were wondering how to make a discreet exit from the whole situation when into the car park drove a large black Merc with what appeared to contain four big black guys. The passenger door opened and out stepped our tall, thin black guy from the club. 'That's him,' Noz and I shouted in unison, whereupon the PC informed the van over the radio to 'Go! Go! Go!'

The van sprang to life and roared down the road and into the car park and blocked in the black Merc. The van doors opened and the uniformed lads charged into action. The PC who was with us was so overcome by excitement he just dashed down the road to join his fellow officers in the car park obviously to join in all the fun. This seemed to be the right time for Noz and me to make our exit and disappear into the night, leaving the four unfortunate black guys in the black Merc to their fate.

I sometimes wonder what was said to the PC when all the dust had settled and the arresting officer, probably a sergeant, realised that the two supposed police officers who had set up the whole thing had disappeared and how could they be traced.

This was the last time I saw Noz for a few years as he worked mostly in west London and I was an East End officer. But for some reason many years later I had to call into a police station somewhere in west London and on entering the CID office, there he was, large as life. Naturally, there was nothing for it but to start off as if nothing had happened and down tools and go for a small and very pleasant celebratory drink, which, as expected, went on well into evening.

For some reason the above story was never mentioned again, perhaps we had matured a little and knew better than to recall far off days when a couple of young coppers had a little too much excitement for one night. A very good friend, yes, a great drinking pal, yes, and will he get you into a whole lot of trouble at the drop of a hat, most definitely. Good old Noz.

Chapter 8

My First Posting to New Scotland Yard

Being in the right place at the right time can be a blessing at times and this was one of those occasions, when late one morning the entire office had taken it upon themselves to retire to the canteen for a cuppa. Being one of the newest and youngest members of the CID, I was instructed to stay in the office to cover the phones. As I sat there thinking I hope world war three doesn't start before they all came back, the door burst open and in walked the Detective Inspector, who looked somewhat surprised by the empty office. 'Where is everybody?' he enquired. 'Oh, no matter, you will have to do,' he continued. 'What's your name again?' 'Woodhouse, Sir,' I replied. 'Oh yes, now listen up, tomorrow morning my lad you will present yourself at C.11 Department at Scotland Yard at 9 o'clock sharp to provide cover for a guy who is off sick for a while, got that?' 'Yes, Sir,' I said, with half excitement and half trepidation. 'It's only a temporary posting but I think you will enjoy it, just keep your head down, listen and learn and when the sergeant gets back tell him to come to my office, OK?'

He didn't wait for an answer but just walked out of the office as quickly as he had entered, leaving me standing there to think whether what I had heard was true or just a figment of my imagination. I couldn't wait for the following day. When I attended C.11 Department, the criminal intelligence branch at Scotland Yard, I soon found out that normally this was a posting for detective sergeants, or at the least very experienced detective constables. The placing of a TDC was frowned upon by most of the officers there, but as they were so short of staff I was put to work on the filing section, updating cards with information on the top criminals in London and the Home Counties as it came in by phone from officers all over London. This was a real insight into the ins and outs of the criminal world as it happened, and although at times it was extremely busy, I did find time to browse through some of the cards, out of pure interest. I was fascinated to come across a card in the name of a guy I didn't know but who lived with his girlfriend in the flat just below my parent's flat, in North London. It appears he was a very active criminal and always up to no good, but there didn't seem to be very much up-to-date information on him. A couple of days later on a visit to my parents, I quizzed them on how much they knew about the couple in the flat below, whilst keeping my cards very much close to my chest, as it where, so as not to involve my parents in any way. But I forgot how shrewd Mum was!

Although she was getting on a bit in years, it didn't take her long to put two and two together and come up with why I was so interested in the guy downstairs. In passing, she mentioned she had overheard a conversation the guy had had on the phone the previous day, whilst he was standing in the communal hall. It appeared he had pulled the phone and its lead out into the hall so his girlfriend in the flat couldn't hear what was being said. Mum, who was on her way out shopping at the time, was standing by her front door round the corner, so she was out of sight. The echo in the hall made it easy for a very nosy, old lady to hear every word, to the effect that he had a 'meet or meeting' at 6.30am in a couple of days at Turnpike Lane, in north London. She thought at the time it was so early in the morning, that's why it stuck in her mind.

On the way home that night I pondered on all the possible reasons for meeting anybody other than someone on the run or exchanging something like drugs or bent cash, at that time of the day.

The following morning at work I had a word with one of the sergeants on the surveillance teams who agreed to set up an operation to cover the meeting. Of course, I left out the bit about Mum overhearing the phone conversation and just said the information was from a reliable source (who better than my Mum), and as there were no up-to-date details on this guy's card in C.11 everybody seemed keen to go along with it. The following morning well before 6.30am the whole team was in place covering different parts of the location in a variety of undercover vans and cars. Everyone was in possession of a photo of the main suspect in order to, first, identify him and, secondly, to record on film an up-to-date photo and who he was meeting. As I sat there in one of the undercover vans on that cold damp morning I wondered how the day would turn out, a good job well done with some good up-to-date information about a good villain or a complete flop? Well, I didn't have to wait long. Within a couple of minutes it came over the radio that one of the team the other side of Turnpike Lane had recognised our main suspect with two others, walking down the side of some lorries parked in a side turning. Before he could finish what he was saying, the radio operator suddenly came out with, 'I don't believe it, they are doing a lorry, no they are nicking it, it's on the move. Christ, they're good, it only took them a couple of seconds and they had it going.' This was completely out of the blue and took us by surprise, a different ball game. C.11 normally just monitor situations and take photos and gain information and are not to be used as arrest teams in order to maintain the anonymity of the officers. But this time most of the team had actually witnessed the theft of a lorry and presumably the high-value load it contained. Yes, we were completely taken by surprise but being in the presence of experienced coppers the whole thing was treated like just another day at the office. As we all hit the road in pursuit of the stolen lorry, it suddenly became apparent that a second lorry was also following the stolen lorry. A check was quickly done on the radio to trace the owner of this second lorry, and this revealed the second lorry was on false index plates. It was time to call on some help and pretty quickly. A call to the Yard on the radio was made as the radio channel we were working on didn't have the facilities to speak to the local police stations. The Yard soon made contact with Wood Green Police Station, and half the officers going off night duty and half the oncoming day duty officers were dispatched in our direction. It wasn't long before we had it confirmed by the Yard that uniformed officers were on way. Within a couple of minutes word came over the radio from the lead car on our surveillance team that both lorries had pulled into a small lane round the back of Haringey, North London. It appeared the stolen lorry had parked up the lane effectively blocking it off, whilst the other lorry on false plates had reversed up to it with the back doors fully open.

There then followed frantic efforts to transfer the load from one lorry to the other by the villains, all of which was recorded quite nicely on film. But how long could we wait for the arrest team to arrive? Things where getting pretty desperate, especially when it looked like they were about to make their getaway in the second lorry, when right on time a couple of police vans pulled into the lane, saving our team the necessity to expose themselves as police officers. What happened next was purely in my mind's eye as the picture was described over the radio as the villains made a break for it closely followed by what seemed like dozens of uniformed officers. The quiet, little lane had been transformed into the scene of a rugby-style cup final with body tackles going in left, right and centre. There were villains running in all directions and being jumped on by uniformed bobbies, but eventually order was restored and the prisoners, plus the two lorries, where taken to Wood Green Police Station, where the villains were interviewed by the local CID. Incidentally, by this time they were aware that the whole incident had been photographed from start to finish. The team of villains including my man all put their hands up and admitted the theft of both lorries and of course to the valuable load of, yes, you've guessed it, MEAT, worth in the region of thousands of pounds. To this day none of the villains knew who the police informant was, I don't know if it helped or not but my stay in C.11 lasted quite a few months after that incident. The girlfriend of the main man, who lived in the flat below Mum, confided in her sometime later and said that her boyfriend had got a job abroad and would not be about for some time, so that's what they call it! You might have noticed that no mention of the suspect's name has been included in this true story, obviously to protect the identity of the undercover police informant.

Eventually, however, I was posted back to Ilford Police Station to return to normal duties, a little more experienced in the world of the CID. Back to more routine work of nicking shoplifters and the like, and before long it felt like I had never been away, the everyday jobs of domestic burglary and car crime became the bread and butter of a normal day, at least for a couple of months.

Except for one particular burglary at an old lady's house not too far from the nick. The owner's grandson was on leave from the Parachute Regiment and had stayed overnight at his grandma's, sleeping on the settee, just under the front window. It appears a scruffy, unwashed local yob had decided to force the front window of the house and gain entry, but as he put his foot through the window he inadvertently stepped on the grandson's face. When I was called to the scene an hour later, I found blood everywhere, up the walls, all over the carpet and the grandson. It was like a war scene. The grandson, a 25-year-old, 6ft chap with a shaven head and built like a JCB digger, was just calmly sitting down in the kitchen drinking a cup of tea. I asked him what injuries he had and if he was hurt at all, but he just said, 'No, it's all his blood.' During my investigation the scruffy yob made a number of complaints about his injuries, but the grandson, with just a touch of instruction, stuck to his story that it was self-defence, and who was I to disagree. Natural justice comes to mind, I think!

Now, whilst I was enjoying myself in the safety of the outskirts of the Metropolitan Police Areas at Ilford, Essex, there was a lot more happening up in town, which at the time I should have been more aware of. For instance, midway through the summer of 1970, an explosion occurred at the Putney home of the Police Commissioner, Sir John Waldron. It was thought at the time to be the work of the Angry Brigade, and caused quite a stir in the press, as you can imagine. Whether this resulted in what is known as 'cause and effect' I don't know for sure, but before long the Army Council of the IRA, having seen the result in the press of the above bombing, decided that because of the British government's policies the British people needed a kick up the backside, by way of a bombing campaign. This started in London in the early part of 1973. Immediately, the Metropolitan Police came under pressure to form a designated unit to deal with the threat.

I would like to think it was my reputation, but if the truth be known it was probably only a case of right time, right place, but in August 1973 I was seconded to the newly formed Scotland Yard Bomb Squad. From the early part of 1973 London had been taking a pounding from the IRA. There was a series of letter bombs and packages going off all over London and there wasn't a sufficient number of detectives to deal with and coordinate the enquiries. So, the Yard, in its wisdom, formed a team of about thirty to forty temporary detectives, like myself, who would use their own cars to collect and transport all the suspect letter bombs and packages reported in the London area to Scotland Yard for X-ray, and if they looked suspicious in any way, they would be handed over to the military bomb-disposal guys. It all sounds a bit amateurish but this kind of situation hadn't happened before. The police force was overwhelmed as there were so many suspected letters bombs being reported by members of the public. Looking back, I don't think conveying suspect letter bombs in the boot of my own car, next to the petrol tank, in a cardboard box, was a particularly good idea. But if the truth were known there weren't too many actual bombs sent through the post. Apart from one incident concerning one of our lads. Instead of bringing all suspect letters in to the Yard for X-ray and later returning them to their owners, as instructed, he decided to open one, to save time, but on this particular occasion it was a real bomb. It went off in the kitchen of the house he was attending, blowing off part of two fingers. It was more than a gentle reminder to all of us on the Squad to be extremely careful at all times. This was a real enemy we were dealing with.

It wasn't the number of real bombs sent through the post, it was the fear and chaos it caused to London as a whole. But after a few months, with fewer and fewer suspect letter bombs being reported, it was thought that our team could be better utilised on the investigation side of the enquiry as things got a bit quieter.

It was about this time that we were put to work on surveillance of IRA suspects and known places where they frequented, together with clearing the scenes at bomb attacks, looking for evidence of the types of bombs used, bits of wire, clock mechanisms and so on. Working all hours, seven days a week, non-stop, I didn't see much of the family and I missed so much, but this was war where people's lives were at stake. I don't know where Sue got her patience from, it must have been like being a single parent for her.

I do recall the Christmas of 1973, when we were quite busy. In fact, on 21 December 1973, I had to take sick leave as Sue was giving birth to Jamie, our third son, and someone had to look after our other two boys. We weren't allowed to take time off work in the normal way, we were far too busy, and I wasn't even allowed compassionate leave. The following extracts from my police duty diary show exactly why.

Monday 24 December 1973
On duty 5am at Ilford Police station and on to Leytonstone, East Ham, Hackney, Limehouse and Kings Cross, regarding collection of suspect letter bombs and on to the Yard re same, on to Wellington Barracks [where we had an office] by 9am, and there engaged in general office duties to 5.15pm, then returned to Ilford, where off duty at 6pm.

Total hours of duty 13 hours.

[6 hours later]

Tuesday 25 December 1973
On duty 12.10am and on to the Swiss Cottage pub, North London, where engaged at bomb scene, to 1.30am then on to the North Star pub, and again engaged at bomb scene to 4am and returning to Wellington Barracks and on to Ilford Police station and off duty at 6.10am.

Total hours of duty 6 hours.

Wednesday 26 December 1973

On duty 9am at Ilford Police Station and on to Wellington Barracks where engaged re general office duties to 11am then to local police garage regarding petrol and maintenance of police undercover van, then to Bomb Squad office at Yard, where engaged. Returning to Wellington Barracks and off duty at 5pm.

Total hours of duty 8 hours.

[5 hours later]

Recommenced duty at 9.45pm and on to the Stage Door pub, Victoria, London, and engaged at bomb scene and exhibits then returning to Wellington Barracks, where engaged to 11.50pm then to Sloane Square Underground station and again engaged at bomb scene, until my return to Wellington Barracks and off duty at 5am.

Total hours of duty 15 hours 30 mins.

Thursday 27 December 1973

On duty 10am at Ilford Police Station and on to East Ham, Kings Cross, Hackney and Limehouse, then to the Yard re collection of suspect bombs and on to Wellington Barracks, where engaged in general office duties to my return to Ilford Police Station and off duty 8.30pm.

Total hours of duty 10 hours 30 mins.

Friday 28 December 1973

On duty 8am at Ilford Police station and on to Wellington Barracks, where engaged office duties to 10.30am then to Holborn, re suspect bomb, returning to Yard at 2.45pm and on to Kings Cross area re general patrol around stations, returning to the barracks on way to the Yard, re briefing. Then on to Manor House Underground station re observations to 1am and on to Ilford where off duty 1.30am.

Total hours of duty 17 hours 30 mins.

So one can see the hours were quite long and exhausting. I recall working forty straight days without a break, then a day off followed by twenty-five straight days before another break. This went on long into the spring of that year.

God only knows how Sue put up with it all, running a home, three young children and a husband who was never there. On one particular occasion I arrived home very late from work one night for a dinner party where our guests were already sitting down. I apologised for my lateness and joined them at the table. No sooner than my rear end reached the seat, the phone went off. Yes, another call out to a bomb scene. What could I say, but I could see Sue's face, she was not impressed, but being the kind of person she is, she just got on with it and carried on with the dinner party, whilst I dashed off into the night to commence battle with the IRA once again. I think if she could have got her hands on any of the IRA that night, their whole campaign would have come to a very abrupt end.

Back then, the IRA did not like police officers in general, and Bomb-Squad officers in particular. We were prime targets, so we were given certain safety instructions, hence the reason for driving home after duty each day and taking a different route, not only for safety reasons but sometimes I got lost, having recently moved house in a small village in Essex, well out of the way and off the beaten track.

In those days police weren't allowed to live more then 25 miles from the centre of London, so in order to get authorisation to move I had to attend the 'map room' at Scotland Yard, to get the distance verified. Well, when I got there, only one officer was on duty, so when he asked me to hold the tape, at one end, across a map of London, about 40ft across, almost the full length of the room, I was only to happy to oblige. Especially when it meant I could adjust the reading by simply shouting, 'Yes, it's just within the 25-mile limit', from some 15ft away on the other side of the room. I don't recall what the real figure was, but I'd already paid the deposit on the house by then, so I wasn't going to lose it now.

The next few months consisted of long hours, sometimes seven days a week with many call-outs in the middle of the night as the bombing campaign took hold. The days following the nights were just as punishing as fatigue gradually took its toll.

However, for a few months I was posted onto the 'clean-up' squad as a little bit of a respite I think. It was our job to get to the scene first and help the ambulance teams with the injured parties. Years later I still get flash backs of those scenes, children covered in blood, crying for their mothers, someone screaming in pain as they are helped from the rubble of a damaged building. Perhaps it's my age, but I still feel an occasional lump in my throat as I remember pulling myself together before going into a detached, professional mode, capable of doing what is required when necessary. When all the injured parties were moved from the scene, we would sieve through the rubble in the search of evidence, which might be useful in the investigation.

Although we were working very hard, we did have some lighter moments over a few pints. We had to turn off occasionally or go mad, as the workload was so heavy day in and day out. This was also complicated somewhat by the fact that I had not only started a family but also joined the Freemasons. There wasn't a free minute in the day to be had. With all the travelling that goes with these activities, those days were extremely hectic. Even our Bomb-Squad office was constantly being moved from one nondescript building to another in central London to keep one step ahead of the IRA, which was undoubtedly also doing some kind of counter surveillance. One night there was a kidnap attempt on an officer in the car park we used near our temporary nondescript office in Victoria, which was once an old school building the 'Met' had taken over! Although this officer was not on the Bomb Squad, strangely enough, he did have the same surname as our Detective Inspector.

It appeared he was a uniformed officer, who was dressed in half uniform and half civilian clothes, stationed locally, who was picking up his car after duty when he was jumped on by three or four men, with Irish accents, in the multi-storey car park. He was forced down on his knees and his hands were tied behind his back, then a gun was put to his head, but at this point he started to cry. It was thought, at the time, that this may have saved his life as this wasn't the action of a detective inspector on Scotland Yard's Bomb Squad, not that that is in any way a criticism of his actions. Who can say any one of us wouldn't have done exactly the same thing with the threat of a bullet in the back of the head?

However, this incident prompted a directive from the top at Scotland Yard to move our Bomb-Squad office within an hour to inside Wellington Army Barracks in Bird Cage Walk. This is just across the road from Buckingham Palace, where at least we had armed Army personnel protecting us and our parked cars, twenty-four hours a day. It made quite a change to be able just to get into our parked cars having left them unattended for a couple hours in the car park of the barracks and drive off whilst not checking them under them for any tell-tale suspicious wires or packages.

On the home front, as previously mentioned, the family had increased to three, not so small but perfect sons that I love dearly. But unfortunately in those days of constant work, I rarely saw them. The combination of early starts in the mornings and long hours made it difficult to find the time to have any kind of normal life. It was just work, work, work. Life was running in the fast lane and although sometimes scary, with constantly checking under the car for anything suspicious every time you returned to it because, no doubt, we would have been under counter surveillance by the enemy. Yes, it was life on a war footing. We just couldn't afford to take any chances, plus watching out for suspect cars following us. One of the ways to avoid this was to go round roundabouts twice, another was doubling back on oneself. It became normal practice, you just got on with it. It became the norm. Although in the back of your mind you were always aware of the dangers, there were many lighter moments. Sue hated me taking the family shopping in the car on the odd day I managed to get off work early. All this going round the block twice and doubling back was just too much for her to take, so she insisted on going by bus! Luckily, the boys didn't realise what was going on.

On one occasion in particular, whilst discreetly following a suspect who had just left his address, together with other officers, also in their own cars, all fitted with covert radios, I unwittingly closed the gap between the suspect car and mine. Unfortunately, when the suspected terrorist suddenly braked hard at a T-junction, yes, you've guessed it, I smashed into the back of his car. The words 'Oh, golly gosh' did not come to mind.

But, true to my training and a little bit of 'Jack-the-Lad gobbiness', I jumped out of my car and immediately remonstrated, in real east London fashion, with the driver of the other car, in order not to raise suspicion and show-out that police were on his tail. I managed to get away with it with this brilliant bit of acting, thank God, as he just drove away, obviously thinking he didn't want to draw attention to himself as I was causing such a fuss in the street. Unfortunately, on returning to my car all I could hear was, 'Woody's hit him up the arse' blasting out of the police radio and, 'At least we know which car to follow, the one with Woody's bumper attached to it'. I imagined every copper in London hearing the broadcast and thinking, what a plonker, but of course the Bomb Squad had their own radio channel, not that this was much consolation at the time.

Then I recall we had quite a few months of observations at Underground stations, throughout London. Twelve hours a day, late and early turns, stopping anybody that was carrying anything remotely suspicious because of suspect bombs being placed inside the stations. That particular aspect of the IRA campaign wasn't too successful. Although we stopped huge numbers of people, we didn't actually find any bombs.

I should add, however, we did come up with an awful lot of unusual things that people carry around, ranging from live snakes to dead cats on their way to an animal cemetery, to the occasional drugs bust. There was even one guy who when searched was found to have cut away the whole of the front of his trousers to reveal all his 'crown jewels' under his raincoat all ready for a quick flash, not a pretty sight. But at least the bombings subsided in that form. The IRA went on to planting incendiary devices in large department stores all over London, which was far more difficult to detect and fight against, as they were often left hidden just before closing time and primed to go off a couple of hours later. The only way to combat this kind of attack was to search each large department store every night before it closed. This was an impossible task and all we could do was to ask the shop staff to be more vigilant, whilst we tried to identify the terrorists by other means.

We were working all hours, day in day out but Fridays were always late duties for us surveillance teams and my biggest dread, because it was nearly always 'Friday night with big Angie'. Now don't get me wrong, she was a lovely girl really, not that I knew her that well. She was one of about five or six young, female TDCs also assigned to the Bomb Squad at this time. She was in her early twenties, long, dark hair and bright blue eyes with more than a hint of facial hair on her upper lip, you could say fairly middle of the road facially, but she weighed in well over 13 stone. Not all fat mind you, she was very fit and muscular, rather like a JCB mechanical digger. If one needed backup in a pub fight, she was ideal, but these particular Friday nights called for something completely the opposite.

It had been decided by the DI to mount surveillance operations inside a number of Irish pubs in the west London area that were known to have IRA 'collections for the cause' during sessions of riotous Irish rebel songs. The idea was to plant us young TDCs as couples into the corner of the saloon bars of some of these pubs to observe who were organising the IRA collections and try to identify them, what motor vehicles they drove and if possible where they lived. Fairly straightforward under normal circumstances, but some of these pubs were strictly off limits to anyone without a strong Irish accent. This is where big Angie came in, she was second- or third-generation Irish, so it was very easy for her to mingle in and around the Irish pub scene. But here was the crunch, being a mere 10½-stone, slim young man, trying to put my arms round a girl 3 stone heavier looked somewhat amusing to say the least.

I always seemed to lose the toss of the coin when we were paired off in the office earlier in the day. I am sure the DI did it on purpose as there were always screams of laughter and shouts of, 'You're safe tonight, Woody, Angie will look after you' came from all the other TDCs in the office when the duties were assigned. All good humour but come 9pm or 10pm at night in an Irish pub in West London, things were very different. Sitting there, holding hands looking over each other's shoulders trying to make visual and mental notes of who could be IRA suspects by their association with the group of collectors. A kind of watching them watching us scenario.

Profiling suspect bombers is not easy, but there are generalisations that can help, such as they tend to work in small cells of two or three, usually from a small flat located in an Irish area, so as not to stand out. They tend not to be outward-going types, so one would be looking for loners with no immediate family and possibly with no form of legitimate income. So, if one had a name and address or some background information it can make it easy to decide to step up the enquiries on that particular guy or drop it and go in another direction. This sometimes produced little situations that one could misinterpret. It was on one such occasion, fairly early on in these operations, that Angie and I got our first wake-up call. We were in a pub just off the main road in Hammersmith, we must have looked more like the 'Two Ronnies' in drag. Having been there for over an hour, it appeared that one guy, who was in a group of men aged from early twenties to mid-forties, which in itself was a bit odd, was taking a more than casual interest in the two of us. I then noticed he was speaking to some of the others in the group whilst looking in our direction. He then stood up and started to walk towards us, which made the hairs on the back of my neck stand up on end. The last thing we needed was attention to be drawn to us. At this point Angie gripped my knee under the table as she had obviously noticed this guy as well. He approached our table and leaned across to speak to Angie, but because of the background noise I didn't catch all that he said. Angie's grip tightened like a vice and I thought this might be a good time to leave, but all he said was, 'I think I am your postman'. Feeling somewhat taken aback, I didn't know if this was some kind of coded message used by the terrorists or if in fact he was what he said he was, but after mentioning Angie's home address, it was obviously the latter. He then offered to buy us a drink, but I couldn't get out of the pub quick enough, so I just shook my head and nodded to Angie and we left the pub. No real danger after all, just an over active imagination on my part. But on arriving back at the office that night, checks were put in place via Special Branch at the Yard to check on the so-called postman through the Post Office internal security system etc. Obviously, Angie didn't go home that night, but had a free, all-expenses paid 4 star hotel, only for that night, of course.

By the following morning Special Branch knew more about the postman in the pub than his own mother. Luckily, he checked out alright and no further action was taken, except Angie was midway moving from her flat in West London, so this was hurried up a bit, and I think she was in her new place within a couple of days.

I recall another occasion when a couple who were sitting fairly close to Angie tried to start up a conversation. I thought I will have to act as if I have had a tooth out or am mentally retarded to avoid chatting. I dared not speak with my East London accent, even with all the noise around us.

Luckily, Big Angie came to the rescue and just gave me a big hug and said, 'He's lovely, he's my little man' in a strong Irish brogue, as we got up and left the pub, just in time to follow some of the group who had been involved in the IRA collection minutes earlier. Of course, part of the operation included concealing a number of others on our squad around the area in unmarked cars, so when Angie and I came out of the pub we could indicate to them who were possible suspects, so they could take over the surveillance from us. We would then make our way out of the area by bus and cab like any other couple, back to the office in Vauxhall, checking we were not followed. Remember, the IRA also had counter-surveillance teams in operation trying to trace our Bomb-Squad office. It was a very serious situation, so we couldn't take any chances.

I believe we did get some good information by these operations, but it was decided to stand us down after a month or two. Mind you, Special Branch wouldn't have told us even if it was successful. They always kept things very close to their chests, and so my short association with Big Angie ended and the memory of the smell of Guinness on her breath gradually faded. God, she loved Guinness. I was never keen on it beforehand and not a drop has passed my lips since the days of Big Angie. I think the other couples on similar duties in other pubs had just as many similar incidents as we did, but of course your own are always much more vivid in the memory.

After nearly eighteen months of this unreal life, and the confirmation that I, together with a few other officers, were now substantive detective constables, my time was up. With great relief to my wife, I was posted back to the East End of London. My tour of duty in the Scotland Yard Bomb Squad had come to an end. The 'powers that be' had dictated this was long enough for any young police officer to be in the front line under that kind of pressure, which, no doubt, could affect his young family. Or could it have been another factor, all that overtime we young coppers were costing the job? You notice I didn't use the word 'stress'. That's a very modern, wimpy expression that means, 'I can't handle life, I've got a headache.' I digress.

So late in 1974, I went back to ordinary police duty at Plaistow Police Station, East London, as a detective constable. With thieves, bank robbers and burglars, plus the occasional punch-up. Life was much more fun and relaxed. No more looking over my shoulder twenty-four hours a day wondering if my luck would run out, as it could have quite easily, and I could start the process of forgetting some of those images of the bodies, some of them children, at some of the bomb scenes, if one ever can.

Chapter 9

A Detective in East London

anning Town, what a place! It was great but hard as nails. In fact, Terry Lawless, the well-known boxing trainer who helped to produce four British world champions but sadly died in December 2009 aged 76 years, was based here in Canning Town during his days as a manager at the Royal Oak gym, above the pub of the same name. This was also near West Ham, just up the road from where he was born. On my arrival at Plaistow Police Station, which covered the Canning Town area, I was given my first introduction to the allocation of crimes from the 'Crime Book'. This recorded all the crimes on a daily basis and also detailed all the investigations that had been carried out on each particular crime. These crimes were allocated to each of the officers on duty at the time on a daily basis by the most senior officer there, which meant at times it was the sergeant.

At about this time at Plaistow nick there was a certain DS Hayday, later to become a friend over many years, who, incidentally, had a wicked sense of humour. One particular morning, a crime was reported regarding the theft of a horse. Yes, you read it right, a horse and, of course, being the new boy on the block, I was nominated by DS Bob Hayday as the investigating officer. 'Where do I start with this one, Serge?' I asked. 'Why not get a "dead or alive" wanted poster knocked up in the local press,' he said as he walked away with a wry smile on his face. 'Thanks a lot,' I thought, but there was a gem of an idea there. If I could get a description of the horse circulated in the local press, I might get some phone calls from members of the public. However, DS Bob Hayday was well ahead of me. By the time I rang the local paper and spoke to the chief crime reporter, who I think was Jeff Edwards, later to become the chief crime reporter for the *Daily Mirror*, he had already written the piece, with the aid of Bob Hayday, of course, with the headline, 'The sheriff of Plaistow has lost his horse. Information wanted on the identity of the horse rustler.'

Thanks to DS Hayday I certainly started life at Plaistow as a minor celebrity. Every door I knocked on for the next week and a half and introduced myself by name, the first question put to me was, 'Have you found the horse yet?' Every pub I went into, the first drink was always on the house, courtesy of the landlord, accompanied with the words, 'This one's on me, Sheriff.' All good fun but every morning on my desk was a supposed clue to the crime. Day one, a neck tie, with horses printed all over it, with a note 'Property found at the scene, retain for forensic examination'. The next day, a horse shoe, in a box with a label 'Preserve for hoof prints'. But the third day was worse. I arrived in the office early to find a large cardboard box on my desk, with 'Red Hot Tip' written on the top in red ink. On opening the box, there it was, a large steaming lump of 'horse shit'. It was so warm and moist the bottom of the box had disintegrated. What a nasty mess, and the smell seemed to permeate the whole of the CID office all day but at least I was getting phone calls. Yes, hundreds of them from every crackpot in the area. Eventually, after visiting dozens of stables, railway arches, backs of garages and yards, I finally found the missing horse, abandoned in a field by Silvertown Way, via an anonymous tip-off. It had, obviously, just become too hot to handle because of the amount of publicity it had got in the local press and had been left in a field.

Now, my next problem was how to get it back to the station. It was a long walk from the bottom end of Silvertown Way, back to the nick and even worse was to come. Walking up the High Road, with this monster of a horse towering above me, whilst wearing a suit and tie, it must have looked odd. In fact, a lot of the shop keepers came out on to the street with their customers with shouts of what I am sure was 'encouragement'. Nevertheless, I was determined to get this bloody horse to the station and ride it into the backyard, but it was as big as a house.

Just short of Plaistow nick, I managed to pull it towards a small wall, which I could stand on and clamber onto the back of this monster. When I was in front of it leading the way, it would calmly follow me but now I was sitting on top of it, nothing I did seemed to make any difference. It just wouldn't go forward. I then resorted to the help of a few slaps on the back end, which seemed to do the trick. The next thing I had to master was how to steer this 2 ton of muscle in the right direction – I found luck was 90 per cent of the answer. Eventually, I rode into the backyard of the nick in triumph. Within seconds every window on all six floors were full of faces cheering and shouting but now the fun was over, how do I get off this monster without breaking my neck? But with the help of a sympathetic PC and to shouts of 'Get your arse in my office, Woodhouse' coming from the Detective Inspector's office, I soon dismounted and tied the horse to a wing mirror of a panda car parked nearby in the yard.

After my explanation to the DI for the somewhat noisy and dramatic bareback entrance into the Yard, I proceeded to make arrangements to return the said property to the rightful owner. Job done! Apart from some rather large heaps of steaming 'rose bush manure' which had to be cleared away, but at least it was an end to the daily clues left on my desk.

As the weeks and months went by, my experience and self-confidence grew to such an extent that I think I gradually became less of a hindrance and more of an asset to the CID office. As a result, I took on more complicated investigations but still had the occasional hiccup, of course.

For instance, one day the DI told me to get hold of a closed in, high-sided dress van from somewhere, so that a number of officers, including myself, could secrete ourselves in it on an undercover operation. It appeared an allegation of blackmail had been reported to him, and, as part of the investigation he had arranged, via a go-between, for the victim to meet the suspect and pay him an agreed sum of money. This was to take place in the Bethnal Green area of East London the following morning, at about 10am. Perfect, I thought, because at that time of day there were hundreds of these types of dress vans about in and around that area, so it wouldn't stand out at all. This was the kind of job you couldn't afford to make a mistake on, as it would eventually end up for trial at the Old Bailey.

On the morning of the following day, sometime in October 1973, I made my way down to the East End of London in the van I had borrowed and parked it up, as instructed by the DI, in a side street, just off Bethnal Green Road. I got in the back and joined half a dozen other officers and settled down to a bit of a wait.

We were to wait for the victim to arrive on the scene later that morning and meet the suspect. Then, at a given signal, when the money was paid to the suspect, we were to jump out of the van and grab him with the blackmail money still in his hand, and as all the bank-note numbers were recorded beforehand, it was all very straightforward. Here we go again, what could go wrong?

As arranged, later that morning the victim walked passed our van and thumped it twice. 'That's the signal lads,' I whispered as I peered out of the back of the van via a small peephole. I could see the victim waiting on the corner. As I gradually lifted the latch on the back door of the van, it jammed for some reason and no matter how much I forced it, I couldn't open the bloody door. Panic was beginning to take over. I had another look out of the van, at the victim, and could see him quite clearly hand over a bundle of notes to a much older, very big, dark-haired man, who then started to walk in our direction. I shouted to the other lads, 'He's made the pay-off, and he's coming our way', but I still couldn't get the bloody door open. I put my shoulder to it but still no joy, and then I tried again, this time with the help of all the lads behind me.

This was too much for the door to take. It sprung open, and I, like a horizontal jack-in-the-box, burst out flying though the air to land, spread-eagled, face down on the road in front of the suspect. Then six charging officers stampeded over the top of me and grabbed the suspect. He was still counting the money in his hand. When asked, 'What was the money in your hand?' he replied, 'What money?' With six police officers' hands holding his arm up in the air whilst still holding the cash, the picture was priceless. He was arrested and taken back to Plaistow nick, where the DI casually asked, 'Any problems lads?' just as I walked into the office, looking as if I been in world war three. The whole office fell about laughing, whilst recounting, by this time, a greatly exaggerated story, which sounded more like an episode from the Keystone Cops.

Mind you, I did claim for a new suit and the van got a new lock on the back door. Plus, months later, at the Old Bailey, I gave evidence, in my new suit, of course, of the 'changing hands of the money' taking place, as seen via the peep hole in the back door of the van, as I was the only one to have seen the transaction, very satisfying. Luckily, no mention was made of any acrobatics at the scene of the arrest or, as the lads put it, a double-inverted pike dive.

Many similar stories of my exploits were repeated at the weekly Friday evening wind-down in the office, over a couple of cans of beer and after the usual exaggeration had replaced 50 per cent of the real truth. In fact, on one of these Friday evening get-togethers, I contested the facts of one of these tales.

It was to the displeasure of the guy who was telling the story, big Dave Whoever, a man of well over 6ft 6in and in excess of 16 stone, with an extremely large beer belly which he used to use to great effect to push people out of his way. Not quite a bully, but very slightly overbearing. So when he moved in my direction with the flat of his hand raised, I stepped back and said, 'Now, Dave, don't be silly I am more than a match for you.' I thought he would just laugh it off and continue with the story, as I was half his size, but he didn't, he just kept coming. I could see he wasn't going to let sleeping dogs lie because I had spoilt his story. So, drawing on all the techniques of judo that I had acquired over the past five or six years at a local judo club, I stood my ground, reached forward and took hold of both of big Dave's jacket lapels. I dropped down to one knee turning at the same time, which brought big Dave's lumbering body off balance. I then gave a sharp tug and over my head came big Dave to land on his back in a dishevelled mess, with a loud thump.

The whole office shook as Dave hit the floor. Of course, he was winded somewhat, which gave me time to make a discreet exit from the office. It was at this time I recall the famous words of the Japanese Admiral Yamamoto, shortly after bombing Peal Harbor in 1941, 'I fear we have awakened a giant from his slumber.'

I had to go missing for a couple of days whilst big Dave calmed down a bit and regained his sense of humour. Mind you, the story did the rounds amongst the local nicks so I gained a little bit of respect, or was it notoriety. Either way I got a bit of a buzz out of it. Not so much for putting big Dave on his back, as lesser men would have crumbled under the sheer weight, but for having the bottle to attempt to do it in the first place. Little did they know, I had had a bit of Dutch courage by way of a couple of cans of beer beforehand and, of course, a blue belt in the ancient Japanese art to assist.

Next came a posting on night duty, which meant, as the only detective on duty overnight, it was my responsibility for all the decisions with regard to all prisoners and crime reports, all over the division from 10pm to the following morning. Slightly daunting, but I did have the help of a police driver in an unmarked car, plus a couple of TDCs.

On the first night, just after midnight, as we were casually driving down the A13 towards a Shell petrol station we noticed a car speeding out into the main road from the forecourt and it had no lights on. There we were, conveniently yards behind it, and from a half-asleep night-duty crew just poodling along the road, we burst into life, like a bullet from a gun, and the chase was on. Down the A13 towards the flyover at Canning Town, reaching speeds of 60mph plus, we could just keep pace with it, until an oncoming late-night bus forced the speeding car to swerve and crash into a lamp post. The crew and I were out of our car almost before our car had stopped and arrested all three occupants, as they tried to make good their escape. It appeared they had filled up their car with petrol and decided to make a run for it without paying. Unluckily for them, the only other car on the road that night was us, an unmarked police car, just yards away. Obviously, it was not their night. Never again would I let the lads in the car have a minute's peace throughout the tour of duty, all had be on the alert.

Of course, this only lasted a couple of nights, then all was back to normal. One thing that did come in handy was finding a new place to have our meals in the middle of the night thanks to our driver's knowledge of the area. We ended up at Claybury Mental Hospital, just off our ground (meaning not under my jurisdiction) but it had a live staff canteen with hot food, all night long. The only thing was because they didn't know us we had to prove to the cooking staff that we weren't patients trying to get extra food. This was extremely difficult as the first time we strolled in, at 2 in the morning and half asleep, the driver, who was known to the catering staff, was gesturing behind our backs to the effect that we were all mad and pretending to be undercover police. I should add he paid dearly for this little bit of indiscretion by footing the bill for our meals that night, which wasn't too bad as they were subsidised anyway.

Some days later, at about 5am, we were about to finish our night tour when we heard a call on the radio to the effect that a burglar had been disturbed round the back of Rathbone market in Canning Town. Would you believe it, we were just five minutes away. It was just about becoming light and, as we approached the scene, I told the driver to slow down and turn off the car lights. I thought to just look and listen. It paid off.

As we turned a corner I looked across to see a lone figure in an allotment area, digging, with his coat hanging up on a post by his side. The scene looked quite normal, except that it was 5 in the morning and you could hardly see in the half-light. This must be worth a closer look. Yes! On closer examination, I could see he was sweating and appeared slightly out of breath, probably in keeping with his present pastime. But as I looked around I noticed his coat hanging from the fence and as I lifted it off, I saw a small crowbar neatly hidden in the inside pocket. 'Not really gardening equipment is it?' I remarked, as I took hold of his arm and said, 'I think a trip down to the station is called for my lad, to verify who actually owns this plot of land.' At that he said, 'Yes, alright, but it was worth a try.'

Naturally, he was arrested and conveyed to Plaistow nick. Still, quite a clever ploy, just to blend in with the background and not hide but be seen. He later told me that at least three other police cars had passed him before we had arrived at the scene. None of them had taken a second look at him. One to remember for the future, I thought.

On returning to day work and normality, although still working tremendously long hours, it was great to be feeling my feet somewhat. That is until one day a new senior officer arrived at the station. I won't mention his name, but he was very tall with a great mop of ginger hair and wore thick, black, horn-rimmed glasses and, to put it bluntly, he made the next eighteen months hell for me. Every report and crime sheet I submitted was retuned for a re-write. Every time he got the opportunity to give me a 'b*****king' he would. In fact, all the detective sergeants in the office would try to screen me from him. It was getting right up my nose but eventually I learned to keep my head down and just get on with it.

Over the next few months I gained even more experience, especially in the field of informants, how to use them and how not to trust them. Every time an informant gave you information it was very wise to check and double-check it by independent sources, if you could, because sometimes they were using you to settle old scores, which was alright, so long as you knew what was going on. It was a case of watching your own back all the time.

In fact, on one occasion an informant of mine was so close to the gang we were watching that his identity would have been blown if I had not pulled him out of the situation and kept him out of the way and undercover for a few days. He was so much in your face and loud you couldn't miss him, he just stood out in a crowd too much, I had no option.

One of those days was spent at a small workingmen's club in Brentwood in Essex, well away from London's East End area, where incidentally Brian, a cousin of mine, was the resident steward. I had to swear my cousin to secrecy but if the truth were known, he loved every moment of it, all the cloak and dagger stuff plus 'working expenses' covered all the booze my informant got through at the club. Years later, Brian would often remind me of that very story with a knowing nudge and a wink as if to imply that he was part of an MI5 operation but at least he kept his month shut.

Mind you, some informants were great, like 'Billy the Kid', as I called him. He was well known in the underworld but had fallen out with quite a few of them and, of course, I was on hand to nick as many as possible, just like my next escapade.

In the early days as a young detective in the East End of London, I clearly recall the first time I was assigned to the 'Q car' for three months. The radio call sign for this car was 'Juliet 12', a very high-powered, unmarked police car driven by a uniformed police officer who had undergone a number of driving courses at the Hendon driving school to a very high standard. They were known as Class One police drivers but, of course, whilst driving the 'Q cars' they were in plain clothes. Our remit was to patrol east London and the borders of Essex to detect and arrest 'good-quality' villains by use of undercover surveillance and informants – a chance to really show my senior officers how this young detective could make a name for himself.

I shall call the driver assigned to this car for this tour of duty Ron, just in case someone knows him. He was a very experienced working copper with a taste for living life somewhat on the edge. It was no surprise, therefore, after a few successful days charging about arresting a few ne're-do-wells that Ron announced we had both been invited to a fancy dress party at his friend's house in Hornchurch, Essex, on Saturday night. On duty, of course, well why not I thought, we deserved it. One night relaxing wouldn't hurt.

We could leave the unmarked police car around the corner and check on the radio messages now and again during the evening.

Saturday afternoon came and Ron picked me up at home as usual but to my surprise he was dressed in a full gorilla outfit. I should have known things were bound to go wrong, but as I settled down into the front seat of the unmarked police car, even Ron's reassuring comments did not stop me thinking, I hope we don't get stopped by a uniformed patrolling police car. I tried not to think of the headlines that kept flashing through my mind – 'Gorilla arrested driving police car'.

Needless to say, my worries were unfounded as we drew up round the corner from a large house, set in its own grounds, somewhere in Hornchurch. Music was blaring out of every window and I noticed dozens of people, all in fancy dress, most of whom seemed to know Ron, as we were greeted by shouts of 'let's get it on man!' and 'Who's the straight guy?', obviously referring to me (which I thought was a bit harsh, as I was dressed as a 1920s' gangster, dark suit, black shirt, white tie and, to finish off, my father-in-law's trilby hat).

Some time later, I think about two hours after our arrival, with glass in hand, as I walked through one of the many ground-floor rooms that were filled with even more and more party goers, I was suddenly struck with horror. I saw a gorilla flat out, on the settee, his head mask partly hanging off which revealed, yes, you've guessed it, Ron in a semi-conscious alcoholic state, unable to speak let alone stand. My heart sank to the floor as I wondered how I was going to get him home later. I removed the keys to the police car from his inside pocket and left him to sober up in the lounge.

Later, as I walked upstairs to the loo, thinking I might as well enjoy the rest of the evening, I heard an almighty banging and crashing from downstairs. What had he done now I thought? But then there was a rush of partygoers on the stairs behind me, shouting, 'The old bill have raided the party'. 'Christ,' I thought, 'is it too late to rescue Ron?', but I couldn't be captured at a party in fancy dress and on duty or stop to enquire from the police the reason for the raid. It was every man for himself. I had to think quickly. This was not the time to be the captain of a sinking ship and stay to be the last one on board. No, I dashed straight into the loo, locking the door behind me, opened the window, climbed out and down the drainpipe, ripping my trousers from the knee down as I went. Then over a garden fence into the next door's garden, over the wall and away round the corner to the safety of the discreetly parked undercover police car.

'Made it', I thought as I slumped down into the front seat trying to brush off all the dirt and muck from my trousers. The famous line from a well-known film suddenly crossed my mind, 'Another fine mess you've got me into', as I pondered Ron's situation back at the house. It must have been a couple of minutes later when the police radio suddenly burst into life and announced 'Juliet 12, contact IR [Information Room at Scotland Yard] ASAP'. No, they couldn't have found out so quickly, I thought, Ron wouldn't talk, or more likely couldn't talk, the state he was in. What could it be, a drugs raid in Hornchurch, where the uniformed lads wanted some help perhaps, God no!

Hastily, I rang the Yard from a nearby phone box to be told that one of my informants had rung the Yard to get in touch with me urgently regarding a job. That was a close call, I thought, but I still had the problem of the unconscious driver, who was probably lying in a cell in custody and, not being an authorised police driver for that kind of high-powered vehicle myself, I had my hands full.

It was a 3-litre, V8 engine Rover, an absolute beast.

So, how do I get the police car back to the police station undetected? What about my informant and why was the job so urgent, and could I fit the job in on my own without a driver? Just a little bit of panic began to set in as all these things crossed my mind at once, but one deep breath brought a moment of clarity and sanity. I thought, let's look at this logically, so after a few more phone calls it transpired that this informant of mine had seen a lorry load of stolen clothing worth about £25,000 in a cellar of a large house, owned by an associate of his, somewhere in Woodford, Essex and it was going to be moved early the following day to a safe house so I had to do something tonight. So, very, very nervously I drove the high-powered police car round all the back streets, just to get used to the thing. Then parked it up not too far from home, nipped in and got changed from the fancy dress into normal clothes. First problem solved!

Then a phone call to the night-duty CID officer covering the area, who quickly gathered up a few other officers and arranged to meet me outside the address of a JP (Justice of the Peace) so I could get a search warrant.

Now I should explain, the night-duty CID officer in charge was an old, seen-it-all guy with a wicked sense of humour. He had arranged for me, a younger and less-experienced officer at the time, to call on a certain lady JP, who, although in her fifties, had a reputation as a man eater, especially where young detectives were concerned, who she often referred to in court as 'My young officers'. It must have been about 2am when the night-duty CID officer pointed out the door of the JP and said he would just wait on the corner whilst I got the warrant signed. I timidly knocked at her front door, not knowing what was going to confront me. It was opened by a very large and very robust woman to say the least, dressed in a garish, bright-red housecoat open to the waist and exposing the largest cleavage I'd ever seen. I introduced myself but before I could draw breath, she promptly grabbed me by my search warrant and dragged me into the front room and literally threw me onto the settee and said, 'Right, let's get on with it then.'

Never in the field of human conflict has a search warrant ever been sworn and signed before a JP so quickly.

Before the ink was dry, I made a dash for the door hanging on to my reputation with one hand and the newly signed warrant in the other. As I emerged into the street I could hear the sound of applause and loud laughter coming from the direction of the night-duty CID car. 'You bastard,' I thought but still, so far so good. Now on to the house in Woodford and the load of stolen clothes. Fairly straightforward, I would imagine, the information was from a good informant, I'd got the night CID to help, what could go wrong? There I go again, getting all complacent.

Within the hour I led the search of the house in Woodford. The guy who owned the house was spitting bricks when I showed him the warrant, but he reluctantly invited us all in. We started looking round the house but could find no trace of any clothing, but instead I found twenty or thirty new car tyres in the loft, obviously stolen, but that was all. So the occupier was arrested and taken down to the station for questioning, but the location of the stolen clothing still bothered me. The informant had never been wrong before, a point I raised with him when I rang him later from the CID office. 'It's in the cellar,' he insisted, but I couldn't find a cellar and I'd looked all round the ground floor of the house. 'No,' he said, 'it's a trapdoor cut into the pattern of the carpet near an old Singer sewing machine in the middle of the lounge.' Now he tells me, so back to the house in Woodford I go to see the occupier who had, by this time, returned home having just been bailed from the police station some time earlier.

He wasn't too happy to see me again but I managed to talk my way into the house on the pretext of clearing up a minor point of procedure so I could examine the floor for the hidden trapdoor.

I should have known he would be standing on it, secure in the knowledge I missed it the first time, but I'd had enough near misses for one night. Strangely enough, I noticed this guy was in his bare feet for some reason.

As we both stood there I casually looked down at his bare feet, and there, just visible, I could see the shape of a trapdoor expertly cut into the pattern of the carpet. 'Oh, you've had an extension built I see,' I said sarcastically. 'Let's have a look.' He didn't like that at all and went mad shouting and threatening to make an official complaint, but I assured him the original search warrant was still in force and could be used at any time and any amount of times within a twenty-four hour period after it was issued. I wasn't sure of this my self but I left him in no doubt that was the case. I pulled the carpet back and lifted up the trapdoor to reveal a black hole and to the left just inside under the floorboards was a light switch.

At this point, I heard a sharp intake of breath from the direction of my bare-footed friend. I reached forward and turned the switch on. There was the missing load of clothing stacked neatly in rows all over the cellar floor, about 5ft to 6ft high.

The occupier was arrested for the second time that night and I had claimed back some precious 'Brownie points'. A good arrest on a night that could have been disastrous. Of course, I had to recall all the uniform lads back from the station to the house to unload all the clothing and transport it back to station, where, with the help of the night-duty CID, we counted it all, labelled it up as stolen goods and interviewed the prisoner again to sort out where the clothing had been taken from, plus what charges to put to him, and set in motion further enquiries to trace the stolen clothes.

This must have taken a couple of hours at least, by which time I had a phone call from Ron, my police driver, who was still at the party, which apparently had only been visited by police earlier that night to ask for the music be turned down slightly.

The party had just carried on though most of the night but as daylight broke he was sobering up and wondered where I was. It appeared he managed to track me down by someone at the local nick who had heard about the arrest and recovery of the clothing, on the grapevine. So, all's well that ends well, but, as you may well have guessed it, not quite.

Later that morning one of the senior officers at that station left instructions for me to attend his office, for some well-deserved congratulations, or so I thought, but it was the officer I didn't get on with, the same one who had made my life a misery for the last eighteen months. Instead of a pat on the back he gave me an almighty dressing down for not finding the stolen clothes the first time I searched the house in Woodford. I just kept my mouth shut, of course, thinking how little do you know, a fancy dress party on duty, unauthorised driving of an unmarked police car, allowing a gorilla to do the same, whilst the officer in charge of the car was dressed in a 1920s' gangster outfit – black shirt, white tie and a trilby, plus an unconscious drink driver and all you can do is criticise because of a slight delay in finding a stolen lorry load of clothing, all down to good police work. You don't know the half of it mate! I dared not even smile during this dressing down, but I did feel rather smug inside.

Mind you, a couple of weeks later Ron, my gorilla police driver, rushed into the police station canteen at East Ham, during a well-deserved break and exclaimed, 'We've both got a Commander's Commendation for a job involving a lorry load of clothing in a cellar but I don't remember that one.' 'No,' I said, 'it's best you don't, the least people who know the better.'

Some weeks later I had another brush with that same senior officer. This time it concerned an incident in which I and another officer were called to the back streets of Plaistow.

An ambulance crew had called for help with a violent, mentally ill and distraught patient. When we arrived at the location, a very quiet and deserted street just off Silvertown Way, we found a man in a very agitated state, who had armed himself with a hatchet-type weapon. As soon as I tried to approach him, he went mad and threatened to kill us as he charged towards us. That was good enough for me, I got the message! Now I could see the street was empty, apart from the two ambulance men, who had locked themselves inside the ambulance. This, I thought, was quite a good idea, discretion was certainly the better part of valour as we dashed round the back of the ambulance screaming for them to let us in. There is something about a man who's lost it and has no conception of reality. He can kill you without a second thought, mental illness is a terrible condition and rarely understood.

Having just made it into the ambulance and safety, I then heard this disturbed prospective patient outside banging on the side of the vehicle with the chopper thing he had in his hand and screaming death threats. I thought for a minute. Only one thing for it, call out the dogs. Just the sight of them would calm him down. The dog section was soon on its way and within a second or two of their arrival they had the desired effect. He dropped the weapon and surrendered himself to the two ambulance men so peacefully, you would think butter wouldn't melt in his mouth. At the end of the day, I thought the whole thing had been dealt with rather well. Nobody had been hurt, including the patient, and no members of the public had been involved. But as soon as this same senior officer got to hear what had gone on, I got another dressing down. This time it was for cowardice. For the life of me, I couldn't understand what he wanted me to do. To go and attack a mentally ill man, possible getting him or me killed for my efforts? There were no other people about at the time, so the question of protecting the members of the public didn't come into it. I just couldn't see the point, but perhaps it was just another excuse to have a go at me.

The funny thing is, about a month later this same officer got promoted and transferred to the internal investigations department at New Scotland Yard, A 10, now known as CIB.2. And would you believe it, he was only there a matter of days when he rang me up at Plaistow Police Station and asked me to join him up at the Yard as his assistant, or 'bag carrier' as it is known. I was flabbergasted. He said I would get a promotion within twelve months, which goes with the job, and he would give me a little time to consider it. Why on earth did he pick on me? What's more to the point how could I say no without upsetting him, knowing what kind of a person he was, he could do my career a lot of damage if he wanted to?

The next day, which I thought was a reasonable amount of time to mull over the offer, I called him back and explained although I appreciated the offer very much, I was happy at Plaistow and taking on more travelling would be much more difficult to and from Scotland Yard. It would mean many more hours, which I just couldn't do with such a young family. He accepted my refusal quite well, thank God, so we parted on reasonable terms. To this day I can't comprehend what made him such a disagreeable person amongst his fellow officers, or perhaps it was me, who knows?

As I mentioned previously, some informants can be very dangerous. On one occasion I met an informant I hadn't seen for some months in a pub and had a general chat but felt something was wrong somehow. So I made a check and found out he was on bail for robbery and therefore I couldn't meet him officially because of the bail conditions. I recorded the whole incident in my pocket book and went immediately over to the divisional office. I saw a detective chief superintendent and reported the meeting and the conversation, just in case I was being set up, which was a strong possibility, as the informant could have made a complaint against the police at his forthcoming trial, just to muddy the waters, as it were.

I recall another incident when I took a phone call from a fairly new and untested informant to the effect that a gang intended to rob a house just down the road from the nick in about twenty minute's time. I just didn't have time to verify anything but my first thought was for the safety of the occupants of the house the robbers were about to attack. A calculated risk, you may think, going into an unknown situation without doing any homework, not good, but I didn't have any other options. Within ten minutes I was on my way with a team of plain-clothes officers, down the road to the location of the suspected robbery. I immediately set about placing the troops in the vicinity, all out of sight and covering all exits, plus a snatch team ready to jump in at a moment's notice. All a bit of a hurry, leaving me across the road, secreted in a shop doorway, as a lookout but in touch with all the units by radio.

We made it with seconds to spare, as I saw a group of four young men walking towards the house in question. They stopped outside for a few seconds chatting then disappeared down the side of the house. I counted a few more seconds, giving them enough time to leave evidence for me to produce at court at a later stage but not enough time to cause any real damage.

I could feel the adrenaline pumping up and down my body. The excitement was unbelievable. The trap was set. I then gave the signal, 'Attack! Attack!' I dashed across the road with one thing in my mind, narrowly missing a couple of oncoming cars, to get in on the action. After a short scuffle four suspects were arrested in under two minutes, red handed but no one hurt. The old couple in the house were slightly shaken at the time but so grateful and all the property was recovered, not that there had been time to steal much. A perfect job, or so I thought, because when I interviewed the suspects later in the cells, back at the police station, they all came out with the same story, which is extremely unusual. It was to the effect that a man had approached them in a local pub and had promised them all a lot of money if they did this job for him, with a cover story that it was his house but he wanted to claim on his own house insurance for some high-value goods.

The description of the man given by all the suspects independently bore an uncanny resemblance to my informant. I know he denied it when I questioned him later that day, but as you can imagine I never used him again. It left a nasty taste in my mouth for months not knowing what he may or may not have done just to get an informant's reward from the police. In any case, I had no sympathy with the four burglars as they weren't forced to do the break-in. They were just out to get cash any way they could.

There again, other informants were great, if it suited them. One particular guy was doing another villain a favour by putting him up and chauffeuring him about the East End of London for a while, as he was wanted by the police. I don't think my informant minded helping his mate out for a couple of days but eventually he got a bit sick of it and told me. We devised a plan for him to drive his car, with the wanted man on board, down one particular road at a set time. I would be positioned there with a number of uniformed police officers doing a casual road check on passing cars. This would divert any suspicion away from my informant.

All went well and, if I do say it myself, I played the part well. The thick copper, not hard to do, who happened to be in the right place at the right time, who insisted on proof of their identity, as he vaguely recognised one of the occupants of the car. This meant arresting both of them and taking them back to the police station, where, would you believe, some two hours later I discover one of the men was wanted on warrant for GBH. I had to leave it a couple of hours to make it look convincing. At the end everyone was happy – my informant, me and my senior officer, even the villain kept telling me I was lucky to be there, in that street at that time doing a road check. Still, there you go!

It obviously never crossed his mind his best mate had stitched him up. Life can be so unkind at times.

Although the hours where much better at a local police station, one still had to work alternate weekends. At times I could split the weekend duty, say four hours in the morning until midday then come back to work in the evening, about 6pm. This, I often did, because it gave me time in the afternoon to drive over to north London, pick up my mother and take her to my home in Barkingside, Essex, to stay over the weekend. Both Sue and the boys got on so well with 'Gran', and it was a pleasant break for her.

One particular Saturday, however, when doing a split duty, I was on the way back from north London with Mum in the car and I popped into Plaistow nick, just to check that everything was all quiet. Unfortunately, I found that there had been a report of a nasty GBH and two people were very seriously injured, and in hospital. As I was the only CID officer on duty covering the area that day, I asked Mum if it would be alright if she waited in the car whilst I sorted it all out, thinking it wouldn't take long. She agreed and as it was a lovely sunny day, I left her reading a book in my car, parked in the yard at the back of the nick.

The circumstances of the GBH given to me by the duty officer was to the effect that a man, who lived in a block of flats overlooking the market in East Ham, had parked his car in front of a market trader's stall, and not for the first time, the two men had almost come to blows. But on this occasion they had both armed themselves with hammers and set about each other, in full view of dozens of shoppers in the market. There was blood everywhere. Of course, uniformed police were called and both men were arrested but due to their injuries they were taken directly to hospital. And would you believe it, to the same hospital, where all hell had broken out amongst their relatives. Also no witnesses had been interviewed or exhibits obtained, a real 'dog's dinner'.

I set to work collecting the blood-stained clothing from their respective home addresses. Both of them had gone home after the fight to change in order to get rid of any evidence of their victim's blood on their own clothes, which police could use in any subsequent investigation. I interviewed witness at the scene and arranged for statements to be taken. I also moved one of the victim-cum-suspects to another hospital. Then just as they were released from their respective hospitals, I got the uniform lads to bring them back into Plaistow nick so that I could interview them under caution and eventually charge them both with GBH on each other and bail them to appear in court at a later date.

All this takes time, of course. Four hours later I suddenly remembered Mum, 'Oh no', was she still alive sitting in my car in the yard of Plaistow Police Station? I dashed into the CID office to find her sitting at my desk with a cup of tea in her hand, courtesy of the station sergeant, who had wondered who this little old lady was, sitting in a car in the police yard. Nothing phased my Mum, she just said, 'Did you get it all sorted, son?' and smiled and I knew all was forgiven. I related the full story as I drove her back to my home, where Sue and the boys were wondering where Gran had been the whole of the afternoon.

Some months later at the Old Bailey my two middle-aged Jack-the-Lads who should have known better, my God, they were both in their late fifties, appeared before a stunned court, having both pleaded guilty to the charge of GBH which could carry a prison term of a maximum of eighteen years. I gave the court the brief facts but when I disclosed the medical evidence concerning their respective injuries, I could see the look on the judge's face turn from anger to sympathy. It appeared that one had almost lost the sight in one eye, whilst the other was deaf in one ear, all down to the injuries they had inflicted on each other.

Having explained to the judge all the surrounding circumstances in the case, I then sat down. The judge looked at them and after a long pause said, 'I think you have both suffered enough, judging by your injuries, so I'm going to deal with you lightly with a conditional discharge but before you go I want the officer in the case to come forward with the court Inspector.' What was going on, I thought, not another cock-up? But no, I got my first judge's commendation for, 'The manner in which the case was dealt with and presented to court'. Having said that, he probably felt sorry for me, doing all that work just for a conditional discharge but I think his decision to treat them lightly was about right.

I enjoyed my life as a young detective at Plaistow Police Station in the East End of London and although it was hard work and fairly long hours, there were lots of good times, most of them, I should add, were in pubs and clubs, seeking information, of course.

I remember one particular afternoon I was with a fellow officer also called John, in a local pub called The Trossachs in Barking Road, E16, seeking information, of course. At closing time, the landlord just said to us quietly, 'Alright, lads, you two can stay on for a bit, but I've just got some publicity photos to take to promote a new lager I've been asked to sell.' Unbeknown to us, the promotion included some scantily dressed young ladies, amongst other things, lying along the bar. Well, by this time both of us were in quite a happy mood to say the least and when asked by the landlord, didn't mind posing with the young ladies, during part of the photo shoot. It was great fun. In fact, at one stage, I was laying full length along the bar, glass in hand, surrounded by an array of dolly birds, posing for even more photographs.

A few days later, in the cold light of day whilst sitting at my desk, I received a large brown envelope, which had been delivered by hand to the nick, containing the promotional photos. Some of which clearly showed me surrounded by half a dozen almost naked young ladies, draped over me like a Greek god, under the headline, 'You should try this new lager, it's got pulling power', together with a short note from the landlord of the pub stating they had been accepted by the lager company and would be featured in the national press within days.

Well at this point I thought, this is it, I'm out of a job for sure this time, back to bricklaying. Unbeknown to me, however, the other officer and the landlord had set me up. The real promotional photos had been taken minus the somewhat unsteady and blurry eyed young detective. After a very uncomfortable hour or so of leg pulling, the true story of the setup was revealed. This revelation was more than gratefully received but I still had to explain myself to my Detective Inspector, who had by now entered the office and was demanding to know what I was doing in a pub after hours in these nearly but not quite compromising positions. I found out much later that the DI was also in with the other two, and pretended to let me off any further action on the production of a bottle of Scotch at the next office function. Lessons in life don't come cheap.

But along with the fun came quite a few good jobs and bodies to go with them (slang for incidents and situations where arrests were made). It was about this time that a murder was reported, down in the dock area of Canning Town, just on our ground. A man had been discovered in the water, with his head bashed in. I was told by one of the 'governors', a chief superintendent, to set up a murder-squad office at East Ham Police Station and take on the role of office manager. This was something I hadn't done before, although I had been involved with murder squads in the past but not actually running the day to day work as an office manager. This was quite a responsible position for such an inexperienced officer as me. However, with the help of some of the more knowledgeable lads who had worked as office managers on murder squads before, I managed to get to grips with the running of the office and the systems needed to keep on top of information coming into the office and what actions should be taken as a result.

The officer in charge of the investigation was a detective superintendent who had a reputation for being a bit of a stickler for getting things 'just right', so I had to be on the ball all the time.

It transpired later via our investigation that an employee of the dead man had spurned his employer's sexual advances whilst out for the day, and punched him causing him to fall back and hit his head. He then realised he might have killed him. He obviously panicked and did a runner but to confirm all this we needed a confession, as there were no witnesses and no forensic evidence to speak of. Shortly after, the employee was arrested and taken to East Ham Police Station, where the Superintendent had set up an interview room. Never having been involved in a suspected murder to this extent before, I asked the governor if I could sit in on the interview and he agreed. What followed was a revelation. To see a man who had such a terrible secret to hide slowly but surely brought to the point, over a couple of hours, when all he wanted to do was to get it off his chest and tell somebody. After all, it was more of an accident than a murder but, of course, that was down to a jury to decide. In the meantime, we still had to go though the procedure of taking a statement of confession under caution.

It was from this and many other similar instances that I became aware of the power of interrogation, realising that it is far better to use a subtle approach, from a position of strength and knowledge, giving the impression to the suspect that there is nowhere to run and hide, but remembering never to bullshit a career criminal because if he ever finds out he will never listen to you again. Therefore, it is essential to do your homework on the suspect himself as well as the circumstances surrounding the particular crime and formulate some kind of plan. During any interview remember always to hold a little bit of information back in reserve as a fall-back position, and always leave an interview with a knowing smile, that always unsettles suspects.

The alternative you are left with is to drag the suspect out of the cell in the middle of the night and take him to the depths of Epping Forest and handcuff him round a tree in a standing position, hugging the tree, then drop his trousers, and stand behind him, so close, he can feel your breath on the back his neck, then whisper in his ear, 'This is your last chance to tell me the truth, or I' am going to put plan B into action'. Not a method recommended by any police training college, plus you may have colleagues who would find this approach somewhat extreme, albeit quite effective! So I'm told.

However, returning to the above murder, I think eventually he pleaded guilty to a charge of manslaughter at the Old Bailey.

Anyhow, it was back to normality and the daily mundane crime book back at Plaistow nick. I knew I'd finally cracked it,

though, late one night, some months later, at about 10pm just
as I and a recently arrived DI were about to clock off duty. As
the DI was new to the area, I offered to buy him a drink in a
local pub, just to finish off the day. Although I didn't know him,
he seemed quite amicable and accepted my offer. So, as normal,
as soon as we walked into the bar of the local pub it all went
quiet; it always did, being coppers you get used to it. 'What the
hell,' I thought, as I walked up to the bar and ordered a couple
of Scotches. The two drinks arrived in seconds and the landlord
said, 'It's down to the lads in the other bar.' As I looked across
the bar I could see half a dozen guys laughing and pointing in
our direction, I recognised them as local petty villains, who were
obviously the worse for wear. Not wishing to lose face in front
of my new senior officer, I said to the landlord quick as a flash,
'Take it back and tell them we only drink doubles.' This soon
took the smile off their faces, but it also put one on the face of
my new senior officer, who just said, 'Nice touch, Woody.' It gave
me a pleasant feeling inside, but as usual it didn't last for long.
And I soon found out why when I went to the loo half an hour
later, there scratched into the paint work in letters about 6in
high, just above the urinals and in clear sight of everyone, were
the words 'Detective Woodhouse is a bastard!'. A bit of a
compliment really, coming from the criminal fraternity in the
heart of London's East End. I had no time for villains generally
especially those who would do anything to get hold of money
including stealing from their own friends and neighbours.

Great days to remember but I had more important things on
my mind at that moment.

Yes, like day follows night, reality had returned again as I
realised I was back yet again in the small bedroom at home,
which seemed more like a cell at times. This bloody chemo
wasn't going to beat me, I had too much to lose and deep down
inside I could sense a feeling that perhaps I might just be one of
the lucky ones to beat it, this thing that was growing inside me,
this f*****g cancer I hated so much. This cowardly disease,
which came from nowhere with such devastating consequences,
not only to the victims but also to the whole family. I'm a better

man than that, I thought, so gradually day by day I began to
come to terms with the sickness, and treated it more as an
inconvenience. The days ran into weeks then months.

In fact, I was getting a bit bored staying at home just sitting
about waiting for the next chemo treatment. I was dealing with
it, I was now eating decent meals in between the treatments and
I could see I had put on at least half a stone, which brought my
weight up to just over 7 stone. But the dread was still there in the
back of my mind when it was time for another dose of that
noxious fluid, I recall feeling the sickness coming on hours
before I even had the chemo injections, my body seemingly
aware what was coming. In fact, on the very last appointment at
the London Hospital as I walked into the chemo department I
had to make a quick diversion to the loo to be violently sick.
When I mentioned this to the doctor, some minutes later, he
said, 'Well, it is your last treatment, so it has either worked by
now or it hasn't, so this one won't make a lot of difference.
Would you rather not have it?' The sense of relief was
overwhelming and I'd certainly had enough, so I shook his hand
and walked out of the front entrance of the London Hospital and
stood on the steps and just shouted 'Yes' at the top of my voice
as I punched the air as if I'd just won the lottery.

It seemed to cause quite a stir amongst all the passers-by
seeing this madman screaming and waving his arms about, but
they just didn't know what I was feeling inside. I was standing
there crying and laughing at the same time, and it was worth
more than winning a dozen Olympic gold medals.

Chapter 10

You Can't Spend All Day
at Home

After a few more months I couldn't stand it any longer, I had to return to work. The first step was to persuade the doctor to sign me off sick leave, but this was no easy task. The doctor wouldn't have it at any price, he said it was far too early! No, no, as if to wave my idea away with a hand gesture, but I then set in place plan B and explained the definition of blackmail to him and how it always leaves a nasty taste in the mouth even if it is not true. He said I wouldn't dare make any kind of false allegation against him, but then he thought for a bit and conceded that perhaps a couple of days a week of light duties might be beneficial to my recovery. His parting words were, 'I am glad we're on the same side of the law, but take it very easy, your body is not used to a normal life as yet.' As I left his surgery we shook hands and I noticed a smile creep across his face, so there were no hard feelings.

The first day back at the Yard, I found it really hard going. The lads insisted on taking me out to the local pub and buying me a drink. Of course, I wasn't used to alcohol, having spent the best part of nine months in and out of bed, so I was a bit light-headed when it was time to go home, especially when I got on the train to travel out into the wilds of Essex. At the end of the line I climbed into my car at Theydon Bois station for the last part of my journey home through the back lanes. On approaching the outskirts of a village called Abridge in Essex I suddenly saw a police roadblock. They were doing spot checks on the odd passing car. I thought I might just get through, but, no, a uniformed officer pulled me over, and asked where I was going. Then he said, 'Have you been drinking, Sir?' Well, that was it, captured on my first day back at work, I then showed him my warrant card and explained that this was my first day back at work since my operation for cancer nine months previously and I'd had a couple of drinks to celebrate. This young PC thought for a moment and said, 'Have you got far to go home, Serge?' 'No,' I said, 'just a couple of miles through the empty back lanes.' Then to my amazement he waved me on and said, 'Take it easy, Serge, and well done on beating the big C.'

He obviously felt a little bit of compassion for me. He must have known I could have been near the limit, not by much admittedly, but enough possibly to lose my licence. Never again will I take the mickey out of my colleagues in the Essex Constabulary.

Obviously, I could no longer still work in the rough-and-tumble world of the Sweeney, so I was reassigned to light duties, but thanks to a certain Chief Superintendent Corbett, who was on the Flying Squad at the time, I was posted to the fascinating world of C.11 Department (or SO.11 as it is now), the Yard's criminal intelligence section, situated just across the corridor from the Sweeney, on the fourth floor at New Scotland Yard. Much had changed at C.11 since my first secondment to this department back in the days when I was a young TDC just helping out whilst an older experienced officer had been on sick leave for a month or two.

I still had to attend the London Hospital every two to three months for a check-up, which included blood tests, X-rays and an examination by one of the consultants, to find out if this was merely a remission of cancer or a cure, if there ever is one. I was told at one stage if I reach five years without a recurrence then you could say I've cracked it. Now over thirty years on, I think the word cure can be uttered but only in hushed tones. I've since been told by a doctor friend of mine that there is only a 0.5 percent 'success rate' for 'Oat Cell' cancer, and that's only up to five years, so if that's not winning the lottery and the pools on the same Saturday afternoon, what is?

So, in late 1979, for the first time in my career, I was driving a desk – but C.11 was just as intriguing as the Bomb Squad and the Sweeney had been, albeit less hectic. It dealt with kidnappings, undercover surveillance and the collection, evaluation and dissemination of intelligence on organised criminal gangs, and, of course, this was my second posting to this particular department. Things had changed a lot over the years, but I was ten years older and wiser too.

For the first few months, my particular task was assembling and assessing the virtually unknown world surrounding the Triads or the 'Chinese Mafia', in London and the Home Counties. My office was in the International Organised Crime Unit, which was part of SO.11. As the weeks and months went by, I immersed myself in the world of the Chinese gangs, 'Wo Shin Wo', the 'Tshui Fong' and the '14K' with their code words, nicknames and secret hand signals. I learnt the structure of the Triads, if there is any real structure, but loosely starting at the top there is a leader, known as 'Grass slipper' or Organiser, the next one down is an Enforcer followed by a Counseller and the lowest of the triad ranks are the Soldiers, known as 'old 49s' who sometimes have personal followers of ordinary '49' members.

Nowadays, the Triad Society as a co-ordinated body does not exist. It has disintegrated into a large number of separate societies all claiming membership of the Triad family but normally acting quite independently of each other. These modern societies might be defined as Chinese secret societies the members of which, bound by oaths of blood brotherhood, are pledged to assist one another and further the particular aims of their societies irrespective of the moral and civil laws of the country wherein they operate. Alternatively, they might best be described as mainly criminal gangs who use the name and fragmentary rituals of the ancient Triad Society for their own nefarious purposes. It's not until one gets involved in something like this that one realises how extremely difficult it is to break into this undercurrent of Chinese organised crime. The language, both written and spoken, the different attitude to authority and the very inward-looking lifestyle within the

Chinese community all made it extremely difficult. So much so, the powers that be arranged for a superintendent from Hong Kong to come over for a couple of months to assist me. Superintendent Chan, or TK to his friends, was an enormous help and compiled a report covering most aspects of the Triads in and around London at the time. Obviously, being Chinese and a police officer working in Hong Kong, he had a greater understanding of the whole situation and could relate to the circumstances in London, as well as being able to blend in far more easily than I ever could to obtain information.

To equate this to everyday life, may I ask what do any of us know about the personal lives of any Chinese people in our local neighbourhood Chinese restaurant? I suggest absolutely nothing, point made I think!

Probing the criminal element of the Chinese community and its murky world of drugs, protection and murder, one found a society where bribery and corruption was considered to be ordinary commerce. Paying protection money to gangs was almost treated as a normal business expense or, as it is known, 'paying tea money'. It soon became very obvious that a white, middle-class European police officer would find it almost impossible to obtain any kind of intelligence without help. The only way was to get some Chinese informants who were close to the action, again just as difficult. Then I came across an owner of a Chinese restaurant, in China Town, who had had enough of paying protection. This particular informant would, however, only talk to me at his home address, where he was safe from prying eyes. He could not be seen talking to an 'outsider', or a 'Gweilo', as they call us or round eyes, meaning Europeans. His information was very useful, but he would only give me background information, no details like street names or addresses for fear of repercussions. The punishments dished out to victims who talked to the police were extremely severe and barbaric by European standards. They included chopping the backs of the knees with a machete to sever all the tendons, making the victim a virtual cripple for the rest of his life, which was a living message to all compared to killing a person, whose identity would be forgotten about in a few months.

There were other signs of Triad participation in crimes that became apparent, such as robbery where not only the victims were all Chinese but when the victims were tied up by the masked perpetrators to enable them to search the premises for cash (it is a well-known fact that Chinese restaurant owners don't like banks). They would usually restrain their victims by tying their thumbs together behind their backs with wire, twisted tight, not only very painful but extremely effective and quick.

On talking to other officers throughout the country it became very apparent this was not only a national problem, from Torquay in Cornwell to Glasgow in Scotland, but an international criminal network throughout the world, rather like the 'Mafia'. But there was one main difference, 99 per cent of all crimes the Triads committed were against their fellow Chinese, who were less likely to report the offences to police, who they distrusted just as much as the Triads. This was possibly a throwback from the Hong Kong police and their reputation for corruption in days gone by.

One incident that does come to mind as a result of the Chinese restaurant owner's information concerned a flat, overlooking a jeweller's shop in China Town. The flat was being visited quite frequently by a number of young men who were members of the same gang, but the property was owned by one solitary, old Chinese man who didn't like the situation but appeared to have no choice but to do what he was told. As a result of this information, I set up surveillance on this flat and observed a lot of comings and goings by known gang members. After a couple of weeks it came to my attention that two rival Triad gangs had been involved in a fight in one of the gambling dens, and although I didn't know the reason for the fight, suddenly two days later the visits to the flat stopped. Whether they were spooked and decided against the job they were obviously planning, or the rival gang had found out what was going on, who knows, but I did learn some weeks later that the old man, although very relieved, wouldn't say anything about his young frequent visitors. In fact, he denied any knowledge of them ever going to his flat, although I had seen them myself on more than one occasion. To this day, I never did find out the reason why the gang disappeared so suddenly. The other thing, of course, was that they may have learned of my operation. Trying to carry out any kind of surveillance in and around China Town was almost impossible! The back streets of China Town were like a rabbit warren, full of dark alleys, leading to dozens of basements where numerous gambling dens flourished for almost twenty-four hours a day, each of them guarded by their Triad minders, inside and out, where the word of month grapevine was more efficient than modern-day Twitter or Facebook. However, because of my commitment to this particular branch of criminality, I was awarded the nickname in the office of 'One Lung Woody', which has an almost oriental ring to it, don't you think!

My new-found friend, Superintendent TK Chan, was not allowed to take part in any police investigation as such because the terms of his appointment to Scotland Yard precluded any such action. This put him in a purely advisory capacity. Nevertheless, we worked very closely together and at one stage he brought his wife Sally and their two young boys over from Hong Kong to see London for a short holiday. This happened to coincide with a children's event I was involved with in my village to celebrate the Queen's Silver Jubilee. Naturally, TK and his family were invited home for the day to experience a traditional English street party. I can still, to this day, picture the two little, dark-haired, Chinese children sitting by my three blond-haired, blue-eyed sons, amongst a hundred or so other kids in the street, shouting and screaming with laughter as they took part in all the games. They took it in turns to push a wheelbarrow from one end of the road to the other, whilst one leg was strapped to another boy's leg in a three-legged race. Then they had to try and burst balloons by jumping on them before climbing into the wheelbarrow to be pushed back up the road, great fun.

That afternoon, whilst both our families watched, there formed a special relationship between our kids that was to last for many years, in fact six months later Sally, TK's wife, wrote to say that her two boys where still trying to persuade her to acquire a rabbit for their tenth-floor apartment, just like their new friends had in a little village just outside London.

She was not too enamoured with the idea! We never did get to know the outcome, although the kids kept in touch long after TK completed his tour of duty and returned home to Hong Kong to continue his career. One parting gem of information he did leave me was to take a close look at some of the Chinese interpreters the police were using at the time, as a lot of them lived within the Chinese communities and possibly, just possibly, subject to let's say slight pressures from certain quarters, which might deliver a somewhat diluted version of what was said in police interviews. Lessons have since been learnt!

It was about this time that I was also proposed and voted into the post of 'Dept Representative' for the Police Federation for the whole of the department, looking after the needs and grievances of all officers below the level of inspector. Quite a busy little number at the best of times.

Within the office of the International Organised Crime Unit, where I was working on the Chinese desk, was another unit looking into Australian organised dippers, or pickpockets, which was a major problem in London at the time. An Australian detective police inspector, seconded to the Yard from Sydney, headed this section. Lindsay Craig was a man of the world, who, amongst other things, had been married four times to my knowledge, a great character, who soon introduced me to happy hour at the Australian High Commission, just off the Strand in London. I recall the first time Lindsay invited me to this weekly event. As soon as we got inside, after passing all the security checks, we made our way down to the basement and into a large function room, where I was given a black plastic dustbin with a handle on the side; this was for all the empty beer cans. I was expected to drag this dustbin around the function room all night long. I told Lindsay this seemed a bit over the top, but he just said, 'Look around' and sure enough I wasn't the only one. Possibly half the guests there that night had their own dustbins, which I must say looked fairly full by the end of the proceedings. Heavy going wasn't the word.

Within a couple of weeks I had two visitors from Perth in Australia in the form of my niece and her friend, on a kind of working holiday, both aged about 20 and both extremely good looking. Naturally, I took them along to one of these happy hours as they were Australians and I thought it would be a good experience. Never again. I spent most of the night acting as a personal bodyguard to the girls, trying to keep the Aussie lads at bay, almost a losing battle I can tell you.

In the months that followed I got to know a number of so-called watering holes with Lindsay, under the pretext of a duty visit by the Scotland Yard Australian Police Liaison Officer. The bars at the British Transport Police HQ and the Royal Military Police HQ all had visits at various times, as part of his liaison duties, of course. In fact, I'm sure he knew his way round London's security network better than I did, and he had only been here a few months; perhaps its an Australian trait, going walkabout in the outback of the London jungle.

Something else happened, as well. For the first time in my CID career, I was suddenly working sensible, almost humane hours. I can honestly say if I'm ever grateful to cancer for one thing, it is the opportunity it gave me to become closer to my young family.

I've always been there for my boys, of course, but the cripplingly long hours on the Sweeney and the Bomb Squad had robbed me of the chance of really getting to know them as individuals as they grew up. I now realise I missed out on so much because I hadn't got my priorities right. This I soon rectified and the love and closeness that I always had for my boys was increased a hundred fold and consolidated with the friendship and understanding that we have had ever since.

When you see your sons after a short absence, do you give them a hug or a kiss? You should. I do! That's why I consider myself an extremely rich man. Forget money that only goes in your pocket! Family relationships are something else. To see a smile on the face of your own child is priceless.

I once saw a plaque somewhere with the phrase, 'Friends and relatives are the fruit and vegetables in the garden of life' and I've tried never to forget those wise words.

Why does it take something like cancer to make you think about what true values are, and what you really want out of life? I suppose it concentrates the mind on the true priorities whilst sweeping aside life's clutter. This new way of looking at life was, I suppose, a consequence of spending so many hours in that darkened room at home, in crippling pain, on my own, pondering on what the future held in store, whilst possibly making outlandish promises to God, 'If I get through this, I will be a better person'. It sounds a bit holier-than-thou, but believe me, it was better than the alternative, that of making a pact with the devil himself if necessary, just to get another chance to live.

Chapter 11

Social Life Begins Again

My determination not to let the cancer get the better of me motivated me to help set up a local junior football team in the village with two other dads, Tom Buckley and Terry Smith. There was no local club for our boys to join, so we created one. Not that I could do much running about, well you can't with only one lung, but being a bit of an organiser I was pushed into the job of transport manager, fixture secretary, league representative, social secretary and bucket and sponge man at the matches, anything and everything apart from running about on the training pitch!

Within twelve months and the formation of a couple more teams, to cater for our younger boys, I also became the club's chairman, which allowed the other dads to concentrate more on the football. Shortly after came the role of chairman of the junior football league that our club was in, and club representative on the local village hall committee, as we played our games there. Yes, you guessed it, before long I was voted in as chairman of the village hall as well; so many hats to wear, all at the same time, but it was a chance to put something back into the village that had helped Sue and I so much when I was ill. I can remember years later a friend of mine telling me that when I was ill he rang Sue to offer to take her to the London Hospital to see me on an evening visit, whilst his wife would look after the boys. Sue accepted, of course, but told him his offer would go on the waiting list, which was running at about two weeks. He was gobsmacked but that's the kind of friends we had in the village. He also reminded me of the occasion he visited the hospital, and on his arrival in the ward he saw a guy handcuffed to two armed, plain-clothes police officers who were just leaving the ward. He asked what the hell was happening, prisoners in custody do not usually make hospital visits but unbeknown to him this guy was one of the underworld supergrasses I had been guarding for the last few months, prior to falling ill. Strangebed fellows, but there you are!

I think it all started with the weekend dances in the village hall to raise funds for the club. I organised them as part of the social side of the junior football club for the mums and dads of the boys. At one stage they were running at one every three weeks – fancy dress, rock and roll, 1920s, you name it, we did it. One thing soon led to another and before long I started arranging black-tie cabaret nights with television celebrities, such as Jim Bowen and Roger DeCourcey (of 'Nookie Bear' fame). Although they were big names, they didn't seem to mind coming out to a small village hall in the backwoods of Essex, providing it was cash-in-hand, and over the course of the evening as long as we made a profit, every one was happy. The cabaret nights were just for charity, not for the football club, as it now had enough cash from all other social events to purchase tracksuit tops in the club colours. We were really getting organised. Then came the fancy dress Christmas football matches between the dads from different roads in the village, all to raise more funds for the club, which was soon running about six to seven junior teams, all of which had to have their own home and away football strips and balls. These events raised thousands of pounds over the years and were great fun.

Then came the club trips to Wembley for the international schoolboy football matches and then it was only a short step to arranging our own international junior matches in Germany and Belgium, with junior clubs over there. Although I had lots and lots of help from quite a few mums and dads, and did I need it, in booking coaches, hotels and looking after two or three teams of youngsters whilst in a strange country, my feet never touched the ground.

As a result of a suggestion by one of the dads, yet another job came up, on top of all the others, that of quizmaster at our local village hall. The quiz craze had just started, and turned out to be a great success.

The word soon spread to other clubs, in and around the area, that it was easier to make money by employing me as a quizmaster. I did all the work, a complete package as it were, providing all the questions and answers as well as running the night, a very loud and over the top compère, dressed in a white dinner jacket and bow tie, assisted by some of the dads who took it in turns to help me. Of course, a fee was charged, which went straight into our football club's bank account.

Luckily, I had a great deal of help from a lot of the football dads, who have remained close friends to this day. As have many of the hundreds of kids who went though the club, who now, years later, still approach me in the village but now holding hands with their own kids and still on there way to the weekly Sunday morning football match. Time stops for no man, not even me!

These were extremely busy and happy times, almost like the old days, except this time I was driving the car of life in the direction I wanted to go in and this time with my family on board. I can't remember enjoying myself quite so much. Every weekend there was some kind of a function going on and most evenings there were meetings, for this and that, and of course the need for even more sets of questions for even more quiz nights.

It was at about this time that a friend of mine, Arthur Albury, cornered me in the local pub one evening and asked me if I would help him out. Naturally, I agreed without hesitation as he was a great guy and every time I had needed a leg up with a charity event in the past he was always there. But as he revealed what he was proposing, I wondered if I could go along with it.

It appeared that Arthur was one of a number of parents who supported a local pony club that offered riding lessons, not only to local kids from our village but handicapped children in the surrounding area as well. They were organising a charity event in the form of a fancy dress away day to raise money for the stables. That is to say all the dads would dress up as fairies and would be dropped off about 10 miles from the stables with no cash on them at all and have to make their way back to the stables by hitching lifts from passing cars. On top of that, they had to call into a number of pubs on the way and scrounge a drink and get the landlord to sign a form to that effect.

The first one back was the winner, but Arthur was always one step ahead and wanted me to pick him up in my car, drop him off at a couple of pubs whilst I waited outside and then take him on to the stables. He would probably be the first one back and win the event, but this was clearly cheating.

I reluctantly agreed. The following Saturday morning at about 11am I received a phone call from Arthur to the effect that he was in a small pub called the Good Intent in Brentwood, which incidentally had a very wide pedestrian footway between the entrance to the pub and the roadway itself.

He told me he was sitting in the first small bar near the door having a drink and could I pick him up as soon as possible.

As a result of this phone call I drove to Brentwood, but I still had this uneasy feeling that what I was doing wasn't really ethical. However, on the way I had a gem of an idea. I drove past the pub and onto the police station a few hundred yards down the road where I asked to see the station sergeant. I explained the situation to him concerning my misgivings and how Arthur was in effect cheating whilst doing this charity event and asked if he would be prepared to help me put things right.

The sergeant jumped at the chance, so we put together a plan of action whereupon he would take a couple of his officers in full uniform and drive up to the pub in Brentwood and park outside. He would then go in and arrest Arthur in front of all the pub customers for importuning whilst dressed as a fairy in a public place, handcuff him and escort him to the waiting police car in the street, where I would suddenly arrive at the scene and save the day.

I couldn't hold the sergeant back as we checked our watches to synchronise the time. Then he jumped into a police car and turned all the flashing lights and two-tone horns on and made his way to the Good Intent pub in Brentwood High Street.

Within a minute I was following the police car up the road, but turned left at the lights and drove round the block just to give the sergeant time to do the dirty deed and arrest Arthur and drag him onto the street. But as I was driving it did cross my mind that I could just walk away and leave Arthur and the sergeant in a slightly awkward situation as the sergeant would not know what to do next as the supposed charge was completely fictitious. Obviously, that would be very unfair on the sergeant who was just doing a fellow police officer a favour.

As I turned the corner into the High Street I noticed a small crowd had gathered outside the pub. I pulled in by the police car and got out, noticing the atmosphere from the crowd was decidedly hostile. I approached the police sergeant who was still holding Arthur in handcuffs and introduced myself as a police officer and a friend of Arthur's quite loudly. I then offered to take Arthur into my custody on a kind of police bail on the understanding I would produce him at the police station at a later stage, which is completely unorthodox and not something one can normally do in real life, but Arthur didn't know that. He was so pleased to see me. And I think the sergeant was as well as the crowd were beginning to become slightly agitated at this point. So, the sergeant quickly agreed to give Arthur into my custody and released his handcuffs to a round of applause from the crowd. Arthur got into my car and we drove off leaving the sergeant to explain, in our absence, that the whole thing was a setup and it was all a joke for a charity event, which no doubt soon returned Brentwood High Street to the quiet Saturday afternoon shopping venue it had been before Arthur had arrived on the scene in his very loud, pink fairy outfit.

Arthur couldn't stop thanking me for getting him released from police custody as we drove back to the stables, and it was almost impossible for me to keep my mouth shut and not let the cat out of the bag. I dropped him off just round the corner to allow him to run into the stables and no doubt claim to be the winner.

It wasn't until much later that evening at the prize-giving ceremony in the bar of the pony club that Arthur suddenly realised what I had done. He was absolutely fuming, almost spitting fire but he couldn't say too much for fear of incriminating himself, so it was very easy to blackmail him into buying all the drinks that night. That will teach him not to cheat in the future and, yes, we continued to be great mates and often retold the story years later to the amusement of his wife Sue.

During this period I went through the chair (Masonic talk) and became Master of the 'Seven Stars Freemasons Lodge'. I was busier than I had ever been in my life, so much for taking life at a slower pace, but there weren't enough hours in the day, and so it went on and on. I had this feeling of trying to pay off some of the overdraft of good will I had accumulated over the last few months of my illness. It's difficult to explain but I felt so lucky to be alive. Albeit I still had the ever-present thought in the dark area at the back of my mind, how long will it last? Will the cancer return, like a wild dog, jumping out at you from the darkness to bite you on the arse and snatch what is left of your life, and a promising career from the hands of success, to be brought to the ground, like a rugby player yards from the try line? But there again, I think its something you learn to live with, eventually!

On the surface, I was the happiest man on God's green earth, what a complete about turn from a life of work with all its own priorities and all its pressures to that of the family man. It was amazing, a new insight into the meaning of life, where I was going, and what for. I came to the conclusion that for a long time it seemed to me that life was about to begin at any time, real life that is, but there was always some obstacle in the way, something else to be got through, some unfinished business, time still to be served, an imaginary debt to be paid, before I could go on. At last it dawned on me that these obstacles were part of my life. This new perspective has helped me to see there is no way to happiness, happiness is a way of life, so treasure every moment you have and remember that time does run out for every man. I remember reading a poem once, which I think was attributed to a rabbi in Chicago, Illinois many years ago, which fits the bill rather well.

'Life is but a journey to be enjoyed, as much as you can, on the way. The arrival at one's destination is merely the end of that journey.'

Meanwhile, back at Scotland Yard's C.11 Department the next few years flew by so quickly. From Chinese Triads I went into the main office where I spent most of my time buried in indexes and taking my turn in the operations room, in ongoing kidnaps and blackmail jobs. That was really exciting, being privy to the inner workings of major incidents in the command centre. I was working back at the sharp end of crime fighting again. It made me feel useful once more, not just an 'also ran' or one of the crowd, but there with input. I was helping to collate and organise information in real time as the money was dropped off at a designated place in payment in a kidnap case or a blackmail offence. Usually in the middle of the night, whilst trying to figure out who was the true victim and the offender, as nothing is quite like it seems.

In one particular case the husband of a kidnapped wife had arranged the whole thing in order to collect what he thought was his share of the family fortune that his wife was controlling, but he forgot the old adage, 'always follow the money'. So, when the same amount of cash was deposited some days later in another account, set up by his brother a month earlier, the two of them came to a very sticky end. But on the night of the money drop off, we, the police, were unaware of the true background of the case and what was really going on. We all thought it was a matter of life and death, so a lot of careful detective work had to be done behind the scenes before we identified the real villains of the piece. That was a marriage that was not quite the same again. Blackmail and kidnap leaves a particularly nasty taste in the mouth because so many times the perpetrator is known to the victim in some way or other.

A few months later a vacancy came up in the photofit section, which later graduated to E-FITs and police artists, still within C.11 branch, but this was slightly different as it provided valuable assistance in the detection of criminals. My new duties included travelling all over London, meeting and commiserating with victims and witnesses of major crime, including murder, rape and robbery, then interviewing them by use of a fairly new concept known as 'Cognitive Interviewing Technique'. In other words, asking questions in such a way as to not influence the answers. It sounds obvious but surprisingly enough most coppers always say, 'How tall was he?' or 'How big was he?', inferring or planting the idea in a witness's mind that the suspect was tall or big. Instead it should be phrased, 'What was the suspect's size and build?', subtle I know but very effective. This way one could get a truer description of the suspect and I could construct a picture by way of a hand-drawn picture or a computer-generated image that actually looked liked the suspect, and all the time still getting the buzz whenever I got a hit on the identification of a villain.

But as usual life wasn't all work. I recall picking up a DCI Roy Ramm, who was later to be promoted to Police Commander at the Yard, from his home address one morning. On the drive into the office, I told him about the previous weekend's fancy dress dance I'd organised at the village hall. In particular, the outfit I had made for the event. For those of you that know of Bernie Clifton, this will be fairly straightforward. Imagine me sitting on a full-sized ostrich, constructed of wire and covered in feathers with false legs, designed to look like my own dangling over the front of the bird. My own legs, in fact, formed those of the bird and stiffened reins were attached to the bird's head in order to support its flexible neck, which was a 4in white, plastic concertina air hose from a clothes dryer. It was a great success.

On relating the story to Roy Ramm on the journey into the Yard, he insisted I bring the fancy dress bird into the Yard and put it in the storeroom. 'What for?' I said. 'Never you mind, just do it,' came the somewhat stern reply, and although I had a little bit of an uneasy feeling about this request, well it sounded more like an order, I knew Roy had a wicked sense of humour so I complied.

Some weeks later, on a Friday night, the female detective superintendent in charge of my particular department at the time got promoted and she decided to have a small celebration in one of the offices on our floor at the Yard. All went well, as the drink flowed, until the arrival of DCI Roy Ramm, who promptly reminded me of the ostrich in the storeroom. I know, but I couldn't resist it.

I approached Ma'am and asked if I might be allowed to bring a 'bird' (slang for a young lady) into the party, She looked somewhat shocked and said, 'I didn't think you were a playboy, I thought you were happily married.' Although she appeared uneasy about the situation, she eventually agreed, and I discreetly left the office with Roy Ramm, as it took two of us to get the damn outfit on, plus it was Roy's idea in the first place. A good twenty minutes later and, fully dressed up in the outfit, I entered the small office where the party was being held to screams of delight, not only from the many guests, but also from the newly promoted detective chief superintendent. This was a great relief, I can tell you, and her faith in me being a happily married man was once again restored.

Then came the news that a group of visiting German police were being taken round our newly completed computer room and were being shown how it all worked. It was a bit late in the day for a visit, but it appeared they had been on a course elsewhere in London, all day, and only came to our department at the last minute. It's funny what a few drinks can do especially when being urged on by fellow officers, so I took the job on and slipped into the computer room, fully dressed in my bird outfit, unobserved by most but just catching the eye of one of the German officers. At this point, I pulled back out into the corridor and away. Little did I know at the time that my antics had also been observed by our computer operator, a good friend of mine. Naturally, he kept quite and completely ignored the outburst by one of the German officers concerning the strange bird that had just casually wandered through the office and corridor of New Scotland Yard's Criminal Intelligence Department. It appeared that the most senior German officer there rebuked this junior officer in no uncertain terms and apologised to the computer operator, saying he must have had too much to drink that evening and to continue as the interruption wouldn't happen again.

I know I should have gone back into the computer room and given the unfortunate officer another look at British humour, but I thought I'd let sleeping dogs lie. But there again, why not, so I opened the door for the second time and looked in. I could see the now-disgraced German officer standing at the rear of the group, just aimlessly looking round taking no interest whatsoever in the ongoing demonstration, perfect timing. I dashed in at the top end of the office, out of view of the main group, in a bouncing movement, as if the bird had a life of its own. I was just hanging on for dear life, making my get-a-way via the exit doors at the far end of the office, when I heard this same German officer screaming, 'Der Bird, Der it is again.' I didn't actually see what happened next, but I'm reliably informed by the computer operator that the most senior German officer took a certain junior officer to one side and gave him a hell of a dressing down. This paid him back for his somewhat smart remark when he first arrived at the Yard earlier in the day and was asked, 'Have you been to Britain before?' He replied, 'Yes, in 1944, but my plane didn't have a chance to land on that occasion.' But no doubt he will swear, even to this day, that he did see a live ostrich wandering the corridors of power in the Criminal Intelligence Department of New Scotland Yard. Oh really!

I was also asked to go up onto the next floor and just have a walk around for a bit, but that was the Commissioner's floor and I didn't want to shorten my career any further, although the cash collection for completing this task was quite substantial. No way could I face the headlines in the press, 'Ostrich Gets the Sack From Scotland Yard'. It's not as bad as sacking a gorilla driving a police car, but still not the done thing.

During the day of course the very serious work of completing photofits carried on. Drawing the pictures was easy enough but getting inside the heads of the victims to get a true picture was very difficult because of memory contamination by virtue of the words used in asking the questions that we had to put to the victims, who were also normally very traumatised and didn't want to remember what the suspects looked like in any case. The human memory is not particularly accurate in times of stress.

One particular case was a nasty rape, in fact the victim was so traumatised I had to interview her close friend, who had also seen the suspect on the night of the offence, to get a picture of him for the investigating officer. From what I was told the victim was a nurse in her early 20s who had led a very sheltered life and had no experience of men whatsoever. She had not only been raped but brutally abused over a period of some hours leaving her in total shock unable to talk to any male officers without screaming and losing total self-control.

I heard later that the officer in the case had made some local enquiries near the scene of the incident with my picture and had come up with a taxi driver who recognised the guy as a man he had driven to Gatwick Airport the morning after the attack from a nearby guest house. Naturally, off he went to Gatwick Airport, where, in the police security department, he spent a couple of hours looking over CCTV tapes filmed in the airport on the morning in question and comparing them to my picture, and would you believe it he found a match. At this point a Special Branch officer entered the office and walked behind him, saying, 'Oh, why the interest in him? I stopped him the other day, he was flying to Ireland. I think I can dig out his details.' Name, address, date of birth, passport number, everything was there. Needless to say, the officer in the case was on his way to Ireland within a couple of hours, armed with all this information.

The following morning the suspect had police not only knocking on his door, in a small town just outside Dublin, but swarming all over his house for forensic evidence, clothing etc. The headlines in the local press read, 'Man arrested in Ireland for rape within days'. I think the officer in the case got some kind of commendation. He said that without the picture I had put together the suspect wouldn't have been identified, so that made two of us very happy. Not quite as good as arresting a suspect for rape yourself but to help in his identification and whereabouts was almost as good.

A similar incident concerned a six-month-old baby, kidnapped by a babysitter in east London. The child's abductor was recognised by witnesses as she was sitting on a ferry boat crossing the Irish Sea a couple of days later. The picture I had made up, with the help of the child's parents, was being shown on television news on the boat. To see the expression of relief on the parents' faces when they got their baby back in their arms a day later was priceless.

At the time you don't think about it much, but it's amazing how many times in one's life that your actions lead to changes in someone else's whole life and, in some cases, very dramatic changes. There are those I've helped to put the pieces back together and carry on with their lives as near normal as possible and those who I have helped to spend the next few years banged up in a cell, blaming everyone but themselves for things they have done.

In point, one further case was that of an unprovoked stabbing of a young girl in her late teens in a telephone kiosk, quite near Tower Hill, in London, at about 7am one morning. She was very badly injured but within a couple of days I managed to interview her at her home, a flat constructed in the actual wall surrounding the Tower of London, in the presence of her father who was a Beefeater, or ceremonial guard to the Tower. I produced what she said was a 99 per cent likeness of the suspect. A bit over the top, I thought at the time, but it was her assessment of the likeness of the picture to the suspect. The picture was duly circulated round all the local police stations. There are a few unusual facts surrounding this case, such as, why should the attacker be about so early in the morning with a 12in-bladed knife, in that kind of area, consisting mostly of offices, shops and hotels, not many dwellings at all? Well, it came to light about three weeks later when a young and keen PC stopped a guy in the street who had got involved in an argument at a bus stop near the Tower of London early one morning. He noticed this guy was carrying a box of large knives, and on being questioned about this, he said he was a chef and these were his working knives. Being unwilling to accept this story as the man had been seen brandishing one of these knives, the PC took the suspect into custody for further enquires. Some short time later it was established not only that this guy worked night duty in one of the local hotels, but it was also noticed that he bore a remarkable resemblance to my photofit picture, which was clearly on display in the front office of the very nick that was dealing with the original offence.

It didn't take much to put all these facts together and, bingo, the suspect was put on an identity parade later that day, where the young girl who was attacked picked him out straight away. Incidentally, the girl's father and I became quite friendly over the next year or two because he was always so grateful for my help in catching the guy that stabbed his daughter. As a result, he was very willing to take police visitors that I had from other forces on tours round the Tower of London in his own time. Quite a valuable contact to have, don't you think? Sadly, he retired a couple of years later and went to live in Scotland.

It was about this time that new regulations were put into force to the effect that after every six months all officers on light duties, which included me ('One Lung Woody'), were to be reassessed by the Chief Medical Officer (CMO) to establish if their condition was improving. If so, all well and good, but if not, they would be retired early on substantially lower pensions. This was a body blow to me as I loved the job, and what else could I do to support my family? Who would employ a man with one lung? It looked very bleak indeed but what could I do? I couldn't grow another lung, I just had to face it and turn up at the CMO's office the following week and collect my P45.

Once again I dodged the hangman's noose, this time by way of an unsolicited letter from a very senior officer, who shall remain nameless but never forgotten. It suggested that Scotland Yard would have a hell of a job replacing me as I was now effectively in charge of their photofit team. If I was to be let go for medical reasons, a replacement with the same experience and expertise would be very difficult to recruit. This stretched the truth to almost breaking point, of course, but a week later there I was seated opposite the CMO in his office, expecting the worst, when he appeared to ponder on a letter in the file he had in front of him. Then he pushed forward this letter from his file making it easy to read, even though it was upside down. The CMO then stood up from his desk and said that he had to leave the office for a moment to take a phone call. I could take the hint. As soon as he left the room I turned the letter round to make it easier to read. I was absolutely astonished to see a glowing report and a request for my retention in the job, signed by a very senior officer indeed. I had to check the name to make sure it was me he was talking about, but even so how could the CMO get round the new regulations?

On his return, some minutes later, the CMO placed the letter back in the file and looked me straight in the eyes and said, 'I'm going to pass you as 100 per cent fit.' I couldn't believe what I'd just heard. Fit with only one lung? I jumped up and shook his hand furiously, knowing that I still had a job and more than that, my guardian angel was still working her magic, via the pen of another man to whom I owed so much.

I was quite at home heading the photofit department at Scotland Yard. Although there were only five of us, we covered the whole of the London area, twenty-four hours a day. This was very different from my previous way of life, all the man-management meetings, weekly overtime returns, duty sheets for the team, in-house training. All of this coincided with someone at a much senior level having a great idea – changing the name of all the departments at the Yard, and in the case of C.11 it became SO.11, and then the head of each sub-department was to put together a business plan, so top management could restructure the future for each department!

What happened to nicking the villains and banging them up? I never needed a 'structure' in the past to catch a crook. So you can see I found the changes in the so-called Modern Police Force, or Service, as it is now known, very difficult to acclimatise to and even more difficult to keep my wicked sense of humour in check. I will explain. In making up the photofit business plan I managed to come up with an overview, an easy bullet-point objective plan. This was thanks to the help of Mike Leverson, my number two in the office, and my eldest son Stephen, who was by this time head of human resources for an international bank and doing this kind of thing all the time.

- Creating greater team empathy with victims;
- Rationalising resources more effectively;
- Amplifying efforts to inform all ranks of our capabilities;
- Pursuing new techniques to achieve improvement.

It all seemed very good sense at a glance, until the document, by this time much, much thicker by the addition of many, many pages of graphs and old doctored reports, eventually reached the desk of an old-style detective chief superintendent, who happened to notice the four initial capital letters of my bullet points. Of course, within days my name, which was already well known to most of the older middle-ranking officers in and around our department as that of a bit of a 'wise guy', was on their lips again, but not necessarily for the right reasons. I hope there was a suspicion of slight amusement on their part, knowing I had bucked the system, not for the first time.

As time went by and retirement got closer, Sue and I suddenly got the urge to move house. Not out of the village that we had lived in for over twenty years, of course, but to something smaller, a kind of hint to all thee boys that it was time for them to fly the nest and make their own way in life, so long as it wasn't too far away of course. And why not? All three were working and men in their own right.

Sue and I found a small two-bedroom bungalow just round the corner, which was badly in need of repair and renovation. I think the boys got the message when we all moved in, about four or five months later. You couldn't swing a cat round never mind put up three grown men. It had a small kitchen and lounge, plus two even smaller bedrooms. Within three days, Stephen, the oldest, moved in with a mate of his from work, over in Putney somewhere, for a couple of months whilst he purchased his first house near Braintree, back in Essex. Whilst Danny, number two son, won £1,000 in a competition, I think on the radio station Kiss FM, which was used straightaway as a deposit on a flat in Brentwood. That was two out of three gone, not bad for the first week, and when I started pulling the house down round his ears, even Jamie, number three son, wondered how long he could stand it before he too had to move in with his new girlfriend.

First came the extension out the back, which doubled the size of the place. I got an old friend round to dig the foundations and lay all the concrete for me. That was just too much to manage but I did lay all the bricks and set all the windows in place, together with the roof supports. Then came the roof structure, which incorporated three more rooms, plus a bathroom, by way of a loft extension. Finally, I dug the new foundation at the front and built a new frontage to the whole thing. That only left the new electrics and plumbing, plus the plastering, which was done by contractors.

It took Sue and me about six months' hard work to convert this small bungalow into a four-bedroom detached house, working weekends and evenings, together with a bit of holiday time I was due. We did most of it ourselves and what an achievement for a one-lung bricklayer and his wife.

Incidentally, every Christmas, I still send an update to my surgeon, Mr Terry Lewis, who saved my life so long ago at the London Hospital. And he replies to the still-impulsive Jack-the-Lad, know-it-all, gobby cockney, whose hair's a little thinner and a lot whiter and is now a Victor Meldrew-type character, although once considered himself to be more of a Michael Caine figure.

Chapter 12

Time to Go, but Where?

Eventually, I saw my time out, still attached to SO.11 Department at Scotland Yard, running the Facial Identification Unit section, and although it was never mentioned, I felt it was about time to relax and wind down.

I think it was probably the hour and a half travelling each way to work each day that finally made my mind up. If it wasn't the continuous traffic jams in town or the pushing and shoving on the Underground, I might have hung on for a bit longer, but I think I'd had enough of working up town.

The day came that I thought I'd never see – retirement after thirty-one years' service. On Wednesday 1 April 1998 (April Fool's Day, a nice touch I thought), clutching my Long Service and Good Conduct Medal (so richly deserved) and a certificate signed by the then Commissioner, whose memory must have been failing as the words 'Conduct was Exemplary' were clearly printed on it for everyone to see, and with a lot of very happy memories, I walked out of the main door at New Scotland Yard for the last time. I crossed the road, turned and fondly said under my breath, goodbye to yet another chapter to my life.

I've often been asked since leaving 'the job', as it's known, do I miss it? Well, hand on heart I can honestly say I don't. But here's the difference, I wouldn't have missed it for all the tea in China, not a second of it, the good friends and even the not so good friends, the situations I've been in, again some good and some not so good, but, all in all, it was an experience of a life time, which in fact that's just what it was, not to be missed at any cost.

Now for the first time in my life I had no job and time on my hands. This gave me the chance to sit back in the garden under the noon-day sun, gin and tonic in hand, and reflect on the early years I gently closed my eyes and drifted into another world when life was so different and I began to recall earlier days. '

As a boy, life was a struggle most days for my parents. Although there were hardships, it didn't affect me too much. Times were hard for most people in the late 1940s and as a family we were no exception. I recall being told that I arrived in this world in somewhat of a hurry, on a very wet and dreary Wednesday morning in September 1944, in a top-floor flat in a large terraced house shared with two other families in the Camden Town area of north London. This was in the latter years of World War Two, when pefabs (previously fabricated building constructed towards the end of the war for temporary use only) were regarded as luxury homes. They were placed strategically in and around some of the many bomb sites scattered throughout the London area and, incidentally, we kids thought they were an invasion of our private playgrounds provided free of charge, courtesy of the Luftwaffe.

A clout behind the ear by the friendly copper was a weekly event, and no doubt richly deserved, not that it was appreciated at the time, I should add. The men in blue in those days were respected and, to some extent, feared by all in the community, including the villains. Behind the backdrop of hard-working families, plagued by food rationing, shortages of decent homes and the undercurrent of black-market goods, I was brought up in a loving and caring family.

One of my most vivid memories of those days was the weekly visit on Sunday mornings to Chapel Street market in Islington, north London with my mother. She was a north-country woman, short and stocky with a lovely smile and a bit of an entrepreneur. She was always looking for an opportunity to make an extra shilling. A trip to the market was a real adventure with the sights and sounds of the stallholders shouting to get the attention of the hundreds of shoppers, the smells of wet fish stalls mixed with the aroma of dead chickens hanging from the side of butchers' shops and the enormous energy of the place.

There appeared to be hundreds of stalls of different types to choose from – fresh fruit and vegetables, second-hand clothing, live pet stalls, men doing all sorts of feats of strength whilst stripped to the waist, then in the other corner, a man standing behind an upturned milk crate with three cards, inviting people to bet on finding the lady, and all kinds of this and that, some legal, some not so legal. It was electric, a kind of a gathering of the whole of north London, well it seemed that way through the eyes of a very small and impressionable youngster.

One of the stalls I particularly remember was the leather stall, which sold pieces of leather, about a foot or so square, for repairing boots and shoes. Mum was an expert in choosing the best pieces of leather, very even in thickness but pliable. To this day I still have the metal last my father used to repair my shoes for school. It now lies on my rear decking in the garden, placed in such a way that it occasionally catches my eye on long summer evenings and on reflection I feel a kind of swelling up inside, which I put down to the result of old age, an active memory and the large glass of gin and tonic by my hand. That reminds me, I must remember one of these days to give it a much-deserved new coat of paint as a little tribute to Dad.

My father was an ex-miner from Sunderland near Durham.

He was a hardworking and occasionally hard-drinking man, who appeared, on the surface, a very self-confident and self-assured person, but if the truth were known, inside he was a man who was anything but. He was very unsure of himself when out of his comfort zone, i.e. the pub. Having said that, you couldn't have wished for a more loving father.

There's a lot more to say about my extended family back in Sunderland, but that's another book. There is one exception, however, a person who was my greatest mate, Bobby Woodhouse, my cousin. Sadly, he has passed on recently, but will never be forgotten. His father and my father were brothers and his mother and my mother were sisters and both couples each had a son, which was Bobby and me, born two months apart in the same flat in north London. Over twenty-one years later, he was my best man, as I was his, at our respective marriages.

School days were mostly fun but having failed my eleven-plus exam, along with most of my friends in the area, I was consigned to a secondary modern school education in Kings Cross. This was a particularly rough area of London where bullies were the norm and school uniform was only worn for the first few days to make it easy for the bullies to pick you out as the first-year targets. Not being particularly academically minded, I just thought other kids were brighter than me in general, but at this time, in the early fifties, I was not aware of the condition called dyslexia. Like most kids of my age who had this condition of word blindness, we were just left to get on with it and wonder why other kids didn't find it quite as hard to spell and read books. Why was it that every time I missed out the letter 'r' in shirt, I was always in trouble? Of course, I didn't find out about what was really going on in my head till many years later when one of my sons was diagnosed with the same condition just before he took his A levels and, more to the point, I learnt it was hereditary. He certainly didn't get it from his mother.

Incidentally, this son is now a senior vice president and head of human resources, global (hiring and firing) for an international company based in New York, so it didn't hold him back too much. I also understand today that 40 per cent of British millionaires either have dyslexia or have experienced some form of it, but back then it was unheard of.

Having put some thought into the matter, I decided very early on in life that it was much easier to become the joker in the class than fight the daily battles with the bullies. It was either that or taking a savage beating most days whilst standing up to them. There were just too many of them. Being picked on by the older boys and their organised gangs in the school, who were bullying and stealing dinner money from us younger lads, was the norm.

One of the first chances to try out this new social position in class was in a particularly boring chemistry class. Split either side of the lunch period, it gave me the opportunity, during the lunchtime break, to purchase an instant-coffee sachet in a local shop and return to school.

The afternoon chemistry period was even more boring than the morning one, so when the class was asked to heat up some water in a test tube with some crystals over a Bunsen burner in order to change the colour to a bright blue, I just omitted the crystals and added the coffee to about an inch or two of water. I then exclaimed in a loud voice, so the teacher on the other side of the classroom could hear, 'Sir, my test tube is dark brown not blue', then promptly drank the lot down in one go, to the cheers of the whole class.

The expression on the teacher's face was just priceless. In those few seconds he must have died a thousand deaths as he rushed across the classroom with his arms in the air shouting, 'No, God, No!' but it was worth every second. Mind you, I suffered a very severe reprimand and countless detentions after school, but at least I was accepted in the school as one of the 'boys' and no doubt earmarked by the teachers as one to watch in the future.

After a couple of years of normal academic school life, we were offered a trade apprentice in the building industry, to run alongside our academic studies in the school. We had a choice of carpentry, plumbing, bricklaying or sign writing. The latter really appealed to me, as I thought I could draw and paint, but I never forgot my father's last words on the subject, 'If you can piss, you can paint. Get a real job like bricklaying son.' So, my tool in life became a trowel rather than a brush, a master mason, rather than a Michelangelo. Unable to apply a few brush strokes to the canvas of life, it appeared my destiny had been mapped out by a few words uttered by inexperience and lack of imagination, nevertheless Dad's word was final!

On the whole, my time at school was fairly uneventful, apart from a few minor scrapes. The teachers were merely doing a job of work, their lack of interest in teaching was only matched by their scruffy and dishevelled appearance. This apathy spread to us kids quicker than nits.

There was one exception, however, Mr Jones, a hard disciplinarian, who could clout you behind the ear quicker than you could blink your eye, so you had to pay attention in his class. It appeared he had been a very good Welsh national boxer in his younger days, so when he learnt that I had taken up the noble art and incidentally reached the ABA quarter finals at the Caledonian Road swimming baths, in north London, he was there to cheer me on. A great character and, strangely enough, he seemed to understand the spelling difficulties experienced by some of us kids. On one occasion, well, on reflection one of many but I don't recall the reason for this particular incident, I got involved in a playground fight after school. You know the scene, a large number of boys formed a circle and we boys got at it, in the centre. The boy I was fighting was using his feet and kicking me but true to my boxing training I stood my ground and continued to box him in the traditional manner. Unbeknown to all of us there, Mr Jones was silently overseeing the whole event from a window four floors up and no doubt enjoying every minute of it. Up to this point he had kept quiet but on seeing the headmaster approaching the scene some distance away from his vantage point, he shouted very aggressively to us boys to stop fighting and to come to his classroom immediately. No doubt we were for it, but unknown to us, saving us from a worse punishment from the approaching paranoid and extremely violent headmaster. Within seconds the sixty or so supporters who had surrounded us disappeared, like the last biscuits on a plate, leaving two lonely lads, heads down, expecting at least a good caning.

On reaching Mr Jones's classroom both of us were expecting the worst but it transpired that I had broken the other boy's nose during the fight. No doubt the result of a very good right cross. I was told to stay in his classroom whilst he sent this other boy straight to the local hospital. On his return 'Jonesy' was absolutely furious and towering over me, he started shouting at me and I don't mind telling you I was terrified, he had a bit of a reputation for hard discipline. Then he grabbed me by my coat lapels with one hand and waving his fist in my face with the other, he shouted, 'How dare you lead with your right fist leaving your face exposed. You're not a southpaw. Jab with your left first then follow with your right. When are you going to learn? Now get out of my sight and off home.' I never did forget that lesson in the noble art, taught to me by a master, in more ways than one.

Some years later, when in my late twenties, I had occasion to enter a pub in north London to find a group of old chaps, well into their late sixties and early seventies, sitting in the corner, no doubt putting the world to rights, and would you believe it at the head of the table was Mr Jones, my old teacher. I just couldn't resist it; I strolled across the saloon bar towards the group and stood by their table. A silence descended over the group of old men as they became aware of my somewhat obtrusive presence. I leaned across the table and said to Mr Jones, 'Sir, would you mind if I buy you and your friends a drink with the compliments of one of your old boys?' He lifted his head and stared at my face for what seemed like ages, but then his face lit up and he said, 'Woodhouse, class 2D. How the hell are you? What are you doing these days?' With great pride I told him and his pals, over the pints I had treated them to, that I was now a detective constable in the Metropolitan Police, working in the East End of London. Without exception, to a man, they all offered me their hand in congratulations. I soon explained that it was all down to guys like my old school teacher Mr Jones, which put him back, quite rightly, in centre stage, holding court, which is where he was when I entered the pub. Shortly afterwards I left the elderly group supping their pints in the corner of the pub, and waved goodbye to old Mr Jones, hopefully having made his day, and giving him an excuse to relate even more stories of his teaching days back in the late fifties and sixties.

This leads me on, quite smoothly, to 1960 when, at the age of 16, I left school and enrolled with Holland, Hannen & Cubits, Building Contractors, in the City of London, as a second-year apprentice bricklayer. This job consisted of four days a week on a building site and one day a week at a technical college.

An idealistic youth of 16 taking an apprenticeship in the building industry is not the most exciting way to spend one's formative years, except for one thing that completely changed my life forever. This was the chance meeting of a young girl called Sue, many drawers above my station in life, who I fell hopelessly in love with. After over fifty years, it's just the same, wonderful, apart from the arthritis and the beer belly (me, of course, not Sue, God forbid!). To this day I look upon her as the greatest gift any man could get, or deserve, least of all me.

We met at the local dance hall, the Royal, in Tottenham, North London, as I recall, on 6 December 1960. This was the days of the rock group the Dave Clark Five, who played there regularly, and would you believe it, Sue also attended the same technical college as I did, the Northern Polytechnic in Holloway Road, North London, but full-time, of course, studying domestic science, I think.

There was definitely a demarcation line drawn between the full-and part-time students at the college. The former considered themselves a cut above us mere part-timers and I suppose they were right to an extent. We were just training to be tradesmen, not taking degrees or diplomas, as most of them were. So it was quite unheard of for a part-timer, like me, to cross the floor, so to speak, in the common room at lunchtime and ask a female full-timer to dance to the rock and roll records that were always playing there. But, on returning to college after the Christmas break, during which I had met Sue, that's exactly what I did, to the sheer astonishment of a packed common room. We made a great dancing couple, but of course we had been practising over the holiday break at the weekly dance hall. To this day, we can still turn heads with our expertise on the dance floor. In fact, only recently, whilst visiting one of our sons in New York, we had occasion to dine out on a luxurious glass-top boat one evening on the magnificent River Hudson lined both sides by a skyline to die for, whilst being treated to a full silver service meal with a small combo entertaining us by a tiny dance floor. Towards the end of a very enjoyable night the combo broke into a bit of rock and roll and, no doubt as a result of the alcoholic refreshment, I took hold of Sue's hand and provided our fellow diners with a spectacular version of jive, British-style. This culminated in a standing ovation from the majority of our fellow diners and, I think, slight embarrassment on the part of my son and his wife, who, quite rightly, think we should be well past all that by now.

Incidentally, Sue often used the term 'Golly' as an expletive. This reminds me of a particular lunchtime back in the sixties some months after we met. Whilst in the site canteen at work, amongst two-hundred or so fellow building workers, I was playing cards round a makeshift table. I carefully examined the cards I had just been dealt and exclaimed, far too loudly, 'Golly'. This breach of building site etiquette was treated to great shouts of hysteria and a round of applause that went on and on. This story followed me, I should add, for some years from one building site to another, all over the city of London. Shouts of 'Golly, I've dropped a brick' or 'Golly, what a nice day' could occasionally be heard above London's traffic, as the comments drifted across the skyline of the City and away.

The next few years were spent learning my trade and growing up on very meagre wages but also madly in love. So much so that every couple of months Sue and I would go out for a meal at a little Greek restaurant in Crouch End. A romantic candlelit affair, we always had the same meal, 'Steak Diane' cooked at the tableside. It didn't do much for the pocket, but it did help us to get through the lean years and who cares when you're that much in love? The memory often reminds me of the scene in Walt Disney's cartoon film *The Lady and the Tramp* when the two dogs are treated to a meal, under the stars, by the proprietor of an Italian restaurant. Ah, memories.

The following few years were fairly uneventful apart from growing up in the sixties when life was all about rock and roll and being a teenager. Sue and I usually went to the Royal Dance Hall two or three times a week, but money was so short living on the wages of an apprentice bricklayer, we didn't get around a lot because we were trying to save up. But as most of our friends were all in the same boat, it wasn't a real hardship. In fact, we had a very good group of friends who were always up to something, so those years sped by at an incredible pace.

However, by the age of 21 life had changed me into a right little Jack-the-Lad and very headstrong with it. I had also collected the wife of my dreams. It had taken all of the preceding five years to persuade Sue's parents that I was good enough to marry her and who could blame them. Even then I don't think they were sure, but as she was now over 21 she could make up her own mind and God knows why, but she picked the bricky with the attitude.

I recall asking George, Sue's father, for permission to marry her and was somewhat taken aback at the time when he asked me if I could keep Sue in the manner to which she was accustomed. I thought for a bit, but all I could come up with was, 'Although we'll never have a lot, I can assure you, she will never go without.' Thank God, that seemed to be the right answer. He then gave me a large cigar to seal the deal but within a couple of minutes I was in the loo with my head down the pan, so much for the Jack-the-Lad image I was trying to portray. Not a good start to impressing your future father-in-law.

As the years went on, however, both Sue's parents realised how much we were in love, so it was inevitable that they just became closer and closer to us, but what a contrast at the wedding. It first started to go wrong on the stag night. I was up in London doing what men do with my best man, Bobby, my cousin. We were drinking in and around the Soho area in London when I realised we were passing a building site that I was working on at the time. It was gone 2 in the morning and many pints of beer had passed our lips, not the best moment to get a brilliant idea, but they do seem to come at the most unexpected times. Why not just climb over the 10ft wooden fence and clock all the lads on for work tomorrow? This particular building site had one of those old-fashioned clocking in clocks that you inserted your employee's card into and it automatically stamped the time on it, 2am. What a great idea. It didn't take much to scale the fence, but all the time Bobby was trying to talk me out of it, but in the end common sense ruled and I continued in my new-found mission. All went to plan, all 200 ghost employees started work at 2am on Sunday 8 July 1966. Then the exit plan, fairly straightforward except for getting over the fence from the inside of the building site wasn't quite so easy. As I climbed back over the fence Bobby grabbed my feet, or so I thought. On reaching the ground I turned round to thank him for his help but there was a bloody great copper standing there. I'd landed straight into his arms. That took a lot of explaining and pleading, but eventually he saw the funny side. Probably he didn't know what to do about the situation as their wasn't any real crime as such, apart from two young lads out on a stag night, who perhaps had gone just a little over the top. He let us go, much to the surprise of Bobby who kept saying, as we staggered away to the next club, 'Why do you do these things?' He was always the sensible one of us.

Then, on the following day, it was a sight to behold, a kind of 'below stairs' meeting the 'lord of the manor'. On my side of the family everyone was done up to the nines in their Sunday best, whilst on Sue's side most of them were in morning dress, including Sue's uncle, Sir James Helmore. Mind you, he came across as an extremely nice guy. I'll never forget the first time we were introduced that afternoon, as I shook his hand and nervously said, 'Good afternoon, Sir' in my best cockney accent. He replied in a very deep voice, 'Oh, just call me Uncle Jimmy', which immediately put me at my ease, something I was very grateful for.

After the church wedding, we retired to the church hall just round the corner for champagne and canapés and speeches until about 6 when the two parties each went their respective ways. Sue's parents and their guests to their house in Highgate for more champagne and more formal celebrations, whilst we went with all my family plus our younger friends to my Mum and Dad's place in Stoke Newington, North London, where we enjoyed the noisiest party we have ever had, well into the early hours.

This didn't seem to bother our neighbours much as a lot of them were 'working girls' and were used to working into the small hours. The same girls who, incidentally, had waved me off whilst hanging out of their top-floor windows half-naked earlier that day when I left for the church.

Some forty years later, Sue and I had our first reunion party for those same old friends who attended the wedding and a good lot of them turned up (minus the working girls of course). Some were not married to the same partners but Sue and I were still together. Every couple of years, we still meet up for a drink in a nearby pub or at our place, to update each other on old friends and family and recall all the exploits of previous years.

One that comes to mind was the 'vicars and tarts' fancy dress car rally, when Sue and I and another couple, Tony and Pauline White, who were our passengers, almost ran out of petrol in our mini. Ah, the old-type little mini – what memories. I noticed we were running a bit short of petrol. No problem there, except this was about the time when self-service pumps at petrol stations were being introduced. Tony and I weren't familiar with these new types of self-service petrol pumps and how to operate them but seeing we (who were dressed as vicars) were in trouble and obviously noticing that the two of us were men of the cloth and needed assistance, help was on hand in the form of a well-dressed elderly gentleman. He got the shock of his life whilst filling our petrol tank as he casually glanced into the rear seats of the mini through the back window, where Sue and Pauline were sitting. What a sight, two young ladies with their knees under their chins with thick red lipstick and black fishnet stockings all the way up to their armpits. Of course, Tony won the day by explaining to the old boy in a very upper crust, posh accent that they were merely fallen woman who we were trying to rescue.

Whether he believed us or not is mere speculation, but he saved our bacon that day by filling the car up with much-needed petrol. Needless to say, shortly after that we got hopelessly lost somewhere near Epping Forest and ended up calling it a day and retiring to an out of the way pub for lunch to the great amusement of all the customers who hadn't seen many vicars and tarts dine out together before. Some people lead very sheltered lives. If I recall we didn't even find our way back to the starting point to book in, so as far as the organisers are concerned we are still posted as missing in action!

Incidentally, it was about this time that Sue first introduced me to a friend of hers, Rod Stewart, in a chance meeting outside the Gourmont cinema in Muswell Hill. It appeared that at the time he was the lead singer in a pop group together with Tony White and a few other friends. Of course, Rod has moved on since then, but he still replies to the occasional invitation to attend reunions at our place, just outside Brentwood.

Chapter 13

Coming of Age

recall that on the completion of my apprenticeship I was duly sent for by the head office of my employer in Queen Anne's Gate in order to collect my signed certificate. I went up to London with Dad and smartly marched into the main office of Holland, Hannen & Cubitts, to be surrounded by oil paintings in gold frames of previous chairmen and chief executives all round the walls. I remember standing there knee deep in red carpet, seeing my father, who I respected enormously, looking completely out of his depth and very nervous when confronted by three upper-management 'suits' who appeared to be very dismissive and condescending in their manner. This may have been a very big day for me, but it appeared to be a mere interlude between golf and lunch for them and it showed. This made me extremely annoyed. I know Dad was a working class guy, as I am, but there was no need for that kind of uncivilised behaviour by people who should have known better and in any case he was my Dad. When it came to the point where my diploma was handed over together with the obligatory hand shake I stopped the 'suits' in their tracks. I pointed out that as I was now a qualified tradesman I wanted to be promoted to a bricky foreman as a kind of thank you for four years of loyal service I had given the company, which I thought was a fairly reasonable request.

This brought on a lot of huffing and puffing and ringing of hands, so at this point I stood up, said 'thank you' and with the three so-called gentleman somewhat taken aback I proceeded to inform then that although I had been brought up in a working class family, I at least knew how to behave and treat other people with the respect they deserved. I then added that I was resigning forthwith in order to take up a new position as a bricky foreman with another company the following Monday.

I then turned to my father and said, 'Come on, Dad, I've got a life to get on with.' I know it was a bit presumptuous and pompous of me but they did annoy me. The look on my father's face said it all. By the time we got outside the building he was bursting with pride, his chest stuck out like a starched Dickey. 'Well son, you certainly told them,' he said, 'but I didn't know you had another job to go to.' I didn't but I wasn't going to let him know that. Work was fairly plentiful in those days so it was no hardship to find another job.

In fact, the following Monday I started work on the site of the old Finsbury Park Empire in North London as the new bricky foreman with my own gang of bricklayers and labourers building a new block of flats, which is still standing today. And I should add it bears no resemblance at all to the leaning Tower of Pisa.

Within twelve months I was a self-employed bricky foreman with my own gang working for me chasing the big penny, or the lump, as it was known then. Unfortunately, there was still no improvement in my accent, much to the displeasure of my wife's family.

Then reality returned. It was the summer of 1998 and I was back at home on the rear lawn in full sunshine when I felt a soft hand on my shoulder, 'More ice, dear?' came from somewhere. 'Sorry, Sue, I must have dozed off, I was thinking of yesteryear.' 'Dozed off? You were dead to the world,' Sue replied, as I offered my half-empty glass to her to be replenished with yet another gin and tonic. Life relaxing in the garden could become a habit; this retirement lark is not bad after all.

A week or two went by and that was enough sitting around, so Sue and I left our newly completed dream house for a dream holiday, visiting friends and relatives. First, to Hong Kong, where we stayed in a flat belonging to one of the young football lads from Kelvedon Hatch, who had now grown up and moved there. He showed us around the island in great style and we attended many functions and parties but after quite a few hectic days and nights time was up. We went onto our next port of call,

Perth, Australia, where I thought my brother and his wife, who I hadn't seen for nearly seventeen years, were supposed to meet us. What a shock when Sue and I walked out of the arrival gate at Perth airport to be greeted by a crowd, the size of a small army, of long-lost relatives and shortly to become new friends. They were waving banners and streamers and, with shouts of welcome, lots of flashes from cameras temporally blinded us. The only thing missing was a brass band and red carpet. Believe me, it was all very emotional. There was my brother, after all those years, standing there in front of me. I just grabbed him in a bear hug, as I felt the tears running down my face. No doubt he was the same. I almost forgot for a moment about all the other people there in the welcoming committee. It didn't occur to me at the time, but what must the other passengers have thought of this old couple getting such a fantastic reception. The next three weeks were spent in glorious heat and sunshine and in even more glorious company, going from one party or 'barbie' to another. We were also introduced to my brother's bowling club, of which he was president, and as bowling is very big out there we were treated as mini celebs. We didn't seem to get time to catch our breath. What an experience, the country, the lifestyle and every thing was so reasonable in the shops, and it was so laid back, except our reception. The added bonus was the very precious time spent drinking at my brother's bar in his lounge, reliving past memories through the bottom of a glass until the sun came up. That happened on quite a few occasions. Again, time just flashed by and then it was time to say goodbye to so many new-found friends and relatives. I'm not a lover of long air flights but at least on this occasion it gave Sue and me time to recover and compose ourselves for the next leg of the journey. I think it must have been at least five hours before we touched down in Sydney, on the other side of Australia, to meet another guy who I hadn't seen for some years. Now retired, but looking just the same, Lindsay Craig, the Australian liaison officer I had worked with at New Scotland Yard twelve years earlier. Although Sue and I only had forty-eight hours in Sydney, Lindsay still managed to show us around the city's tourist spots whilst consuming large quantities of Australian beer. No change there! We eventually retired to our hotel room later that evening to down even more alcohol, in the shape of a bottle of duty free Scotch, reminiscent of days gone by. Like most old coppers when old memories are enriched by the telling of stories of yesteryear, eventually the capacity to stand takes second place to the request of 'alright one last drop for the road', before crashing into a chair to spend the remaining hours in a deep and very affectionate sleep.

Next stop, Los Angeles in the US of A, where Sue and I spent one of the greatest days a child (or old person) could ever wish for, in fairy land or, to give it its proper title, the MGM film studios. There is so much to see of this world of fantasy, but we could only spend a day there. I wondered whether we could return in the future, perhaps with the grandkids, and relive the whole experience again.

And now for the last leg of the tour, Toronto in Canada. Remember the name Lenny Foul, the man who got me out of trouble by getting me into the morris-dancing team in the pub in Essex so many years ago? Well, he emigrated to Toronto a few years ago. He was so pleased to see us during our visit that he arranged several trips, including a helicopter flight over the city. Niagara Falls, what a sight! Then on to a very large Irish-themed pub for dinner that night, one of many I should add. We had a great evening listening to a live ceilidh band whilst relating many stories including the morris-dancing episode to Len's new wife, Bridget, now sadly passed on, as a result of cancer unfortunately. Anyhow, many pints of beer later, whilst returning from the loo . . . yes, I know I've told you the story before, but still it's a great story.

After twenty-odd years the morris-dancing story was still following me, even round the world. There I stood in the middle of an Irish pub on the other side of the world in front of a strange audience, waving my hand keys in the air in a world of my own to the applause of fellow drunks. The only thing missing was the rest of the lads from Scotland Yard's Flying Squad Morris Dancing Team. What a fitting conclusion to a fantastic holiday.

Chapter 14

A New Life

Then, back home with a bump. It took me about three weeks to realise that I wasn't over fond of sitting about watching daytime TV so I bought a small white van and returned, after thirty-one years, to the building trade doing odd jobs locally. Just a hobby, you understand, two days a week, to keep my hand in and get a bit of beer money, and of course to keep fit. A couple of years on, it has turned into a thriving business, still doing the odd jobs, but mostly full renovations. Danny, number two son, was in charge of finding and purchasing the properties, whilst Jamie, number three son, and I did all the work on them. Thus turning them from old shacks into desirable detached family homes, usually at a considerable profit.

Then, in late 2003, a great surprise and something I've always been interested in, but thought would never be within my grasp especially coming from my humble background. Having been nominated, proposed and seconded, I got an invitation to attend the Guild Hall in the City of London. So on 3 November 2003, I, together with Sue and the three boys, accompanied by their young ladies, travelled up to London where in a small hall put aside for such occasions in the Chamber of the Guild Hall, in the City of London, I was admitted into and given the 'Freedom of the City of London' by the Sheriff of the City. Now that's not bad for a Jack-the-Lad gobby cockney. Mum and Dad would have been so proud if they were still alive but alas that wasn't to be. So, life is not always a long line of Mondays when you retire, and in my case it was anything but.

Having completed building number two son's own five-bedroom detached house, which I should add he sold for nearly half a million within weeks of the completion, I now consider myself fortunate if I get Sundays off. Now, I'm on the next project, renovating our present bungalow just round the corner from our original one. Just taking the back out a couple of metres and adding a large bedroom and bathroom upstairs, rewiring top to bottom and of course redecorating in the manner to which Sue has become accustomed. She just rolls her eyes and tells me I've come full circle but, of course, she's wrong, or have I just come back to square one?

Of course, life still goes on, he said under his breath. Other projects come and go; other houses to build and renovate and still more holidays to take round the world. The fourth tour included Tokyo and Fiji and then on to San Francisco on the east coast of America, to return home just in time to greet some American friends we had met a couple of years previously on a paddle steamer going up the Murray River near Adelaide in Oz. They stayed a few days with us before continuing on to Europe. We've since been over to see them in Vermont, north of New York. I think you must agree there are not many who have been so fortunate in life. Not with cash, I agree, but with lorry loads of memories helped with a slight sprinkling of luck dust.

Still struggling to lift the occasional RSJ steel beam on the odd renovation with one lung (whilst hoping not to pass wind under the strain), but I can still go the distance on the dance floor with Sue at a party.

This has been my story, or a part of it, a few brush strokes on the canvas of life. I hope you enjoyed the read. Still a gobby cockney, but instead of a Jack-the-Lad more of a cranky, old geezer, who now passes his time as a parish councillor checking on the opening and closing times of the local pubs, from the inside, of course. I hope one day when my grandchildren are asked, 'Did you know your granddads?' they will reply, 'Yes, a normal one and a nut case.' Thank God I'm not the normal one.